Reprints of Economic Classics

TRACTS

ON SUNDRY TOPICS OF

POLITICAL ECONOMY

[OLIVER PUTNAM]

TRACTS

ON

SUNDRY TOPICS

OF

POLITICAL ECONOMY

[1834]

REPRINTS OF ECONOMIC CLASSICS

AUGUSTUS M. KELLEY · PUBLISHERS
NEW YORK 1970

First Edition 1834
(Boston: Russell, Odiorne & Company, 1834)

Reprinted 1970 by
AUGUSTUS M. KELLEY · PUBLISHERS
REPRINTS OF ECONOMIC CLASSICS
New York New York 10001

. . . .

S B N 678 00600 8

L C N 68 56567

. . . .

PRINTED IN THE UNITED STATES OF AMERICA
by SENTRY PRESS, NEW YORK, N. Y. 10019

TRACTS

ON

SUNDRY TOPICS

OF

POLITICAL ECONOMY.

BOSTON:
RUSSELL, ODIORNE, AND COMPANY.
1834.

ADVERTISEMENT.

THESE Tracts were written by the late OLIVER PUTNAM, of Boston. Part of them were published during his life-time; and the whole are now collected, and printed in their present form, pursuant to his directions.

The Author was born at Newburyport, and died at Hampstead, in the 48th year of his age. Having attained independence at an early age, by successful commercial speculations, and being without the responsibilities of a family, he devoted his leisure to the assiduous cultivation of his mind. This course of life was promoted, also, by the feebleness of his health; which prevented his becoming fixed in any particular occupation, and compelled him, for the advantage of a change of climate, to travel in various countries of Europe and America. Had it been otherwise, the independence and integrity of his character, his sound judgment, his extensive practical knowledge, his high moral feeling, and his intimate acquaintance with the science of politics and political economy, would have raised him to public usefulness and distinction.

He devised a considerable portion of his estate in trust, to constitute a fund of fifty thousand dollars, for the foundation and support of a free English school in the place of his birth; requiring the 'youth to be instructed in reading, writing and arithmetic, and particularly in the English language, and in those branches of knowledge necessary to the correct management of the ordinary affairs of life, whether public or private, but *not* in the dead languages.' His views, in this respect, were governed by a strong conviction of the greater general value, at the present time, of a practical education, in comparison with the mode and objects of teaching handed down to us from a less intelligent age. His munificent bequest will probably take effect in four or five years, and, if such an institution as he contemplated be well established and conducted, it cannot fail to prove a signal public blessing.

He was early instrumental in furthering the establishment of manufactures in New England. These Tracts were composed by him, with particular reference to the questions of public economy growing out of the protection of domestic industry by duties on imports; and they exhibit his views of the policy proper to the interests of the United States.

In these pieces, he aimed to show that the practical school of political economy, and that only, was founded upon true theoretical principles. Especially, he endeavored to give, not only a compendious and practical view of the great maxims of political economy, but a view of them suited to the condition of his own country; feeling that much of the error in these points prevailing among us, arose from the hasty adoption of transatlantic opinions, founded altogether upon observation confined to Europe.

TABLE OF CONTENTS.

SUMMARY

OF THE

PRINCIPLES OF POLITICAL ECONOMY.

I. WEALTH.

As human wants increase, in the progress of man from his primitive state towards that of civilization, so must his labor for their supply increase with them.

With the increase of his labor, habits of industry are formed, the land is improved, the arts arise and are advanced, production is increased, wealth is accumulated, and each successive generation is thus supplied with additional means of accelerating production and increasing wealth.

Individual wealth is that, whatever it may consist in, which gives the possessor of it, in all places within the sphere of civilization, and at all times, in sickness as well as in health, a command over all objects, whether of necessity or desire, which are of an exchangeable nature.

National wealth is not the aggregate of individual wealth, inasmuch as this in part consists in public and private debt.

But national wealth consists of the aggregate of public, private, and corporate property, so far as this is composed of material things having a real and inherent value, and of property in debts due from abroad: deduct, from the sum total of this aggregate property, the amount of public, corporate, and private debt, which the nation owes abroad, and the balance is the amount of national wealth.

Although a portion of individual wealth enters to make up the aggregate of national wealth, namely, that portion which consists in material objects of intrinsic value and of debts due from abroad; yet it does not follow that every accession to individual wealth is an augmentation of national wealth, or that what promotes the interest of an individual must necessarily promote that of the public.

Individual fortune may arise from speculation, or transactions which produce a gain to one from the loss of another, but by which the nation is none the richer.

As the productive industry of the nation is the source of its wealth, transactions and operations which discourage it, however individually profitable, are prejudicial to the public interests; whereas those pursuits, transactions, and operations, which encourage and promote industry, are such as are most conducive to the public prosperity and wealth.

II. CAPITAL.

Capital is either fixed or circulating, and is that portion of wealth, which is employed by the productive classes in the community, for the purposes of income and profit.

The means employed by productive industry, in production, consist in land, live stock, rude materials, the powers of nature, and products; and so far as these means are individually appropriated they are collectively called capital.

Property in any of these objects, if unemployed, or only employed for pleasure, is not called capital. It is then, if spoken of in the abstract, called wealth; or if spoken of in respect of its ownership, it is called property simply.

Capital conduces greatly to increase the power of productive industry; and the different branches of it are more or less productive, in proportion as capital is made to perform more or less of the work in the process of production.

In agriculture, the fertility of the soil and the implements of husbandry;—in the fisheries, the vessels, boats, and fishing-tackle;—in manufactures, the machinery, and the powers of nature, by which it is made to work;—in the mechanic arts, the tools of the workmen;—and in commerce, the money which takes off the surplus products of the preceding branches, and replaces to them the cost of production with a profit, together with the shipping employed in the transport and distribution of these products:—all afford exemplifications of the manner in which capital operates to facilitate and accelerate production.

With the increase of production, circulating capital is first increased; and as this increases, so does the income, and with that the value of fixed capital increases.

These two kinds of capital are not convertible into each other by the simple exchange of one for the other. When a merchant quits trade and enters into manufacture, he does not thereby convert his circulating capital into fixed; his circulating capital goes into other hands, and he gets a fixed capital in manufacture in exchange for it. So when a farmer enters into trade, or a trader into agriculture, they do not transfer their capitals from one employment to the other; but their capitals acquire other owners, and remain as before, while they acquire other capitals in exchange.

It is not by exchanging capital in one employment for capital in another, that the profits of capital in different employments are equalized; but it is through the employment of labor, by which the relative quantities of the different capitals are changed, that the profits on the different employments of them find their level.

When capital in manufacture yields more income than capital in commerce, the commercial capital is employed through the means of labor to increase the manufacturing capital, until the incomes from both become equal. But though the manufacturing capital is augmented by these means, the general circulating capital is not thereby diminished. The money paid for labor is not consumed; and the necessary consumption of the laborer is the same as though he were not thus employed.

The income from fixed capital is increased by the increase in quantity of all those commodities of which the circulating capital is composed, and it is reduced by the reduction of these commodities.

The value of fixed capital, or its nominal amount, rises and falls with the rise and fall of its income.

It therefore follows that every person, whose capital is in real estate, or fixed property, is interested in encouraging the production of exchangeable commodities in all branches of industry, as *the only means* by which the incomes of their estates can be increased, and, with the increase of the incomes, the value of the estates enhanced.

And the most effectual means of encouraging to increased production in existing branches, are by promoting the establishment of new ones, which will excite to greater activity in all.

III. UTILITY, VALUE, AND PRICE.

Things may possess utility; but unless they are objects of exchange, they have no value.

The value of things arises from exchange; and the value of any particular article is estimated by the quantities of other articles at large, which it will purchase.

The price of an article is its value estimated in money, or the quantity of money it will command.

It is by price, which denotes the value of things in relation to money, that we compare the money-value of one thing with another, and thus determine the relative value of each.

Practically, there is only this kind of value, and this kind of price, known in the estimation of things. Commodities are exchanged for each other at their relative values, and they are exchanged for money at their actual prices.

To the possessor, the utility of an article depends upon his own use of it, and its value and price depend upon the want which others may have for it, and what they are willing to give for it.

Between want and supply arises demand, and according as want or supply may predominate, demand will increase or diminish, and the value of things rise or fall proportionately.

Wants multiply with the means of satisfying them ; wherefore, in the general increase of commodities, which supply these means, the demand for any one kind, the quantity of which may remain stationary, will be augmented, and the value of it consequently enhanced.

The variations in the demand for consumable commodities are according as the present and prospective production may exceed, or fall short of, the quantities required for the supply of the present and prospective consumption.

And the variations in the demand for things of an unconsumable nature, as land, houses, money, and so forth, are according as the quantities which come into the market may exceed or fall short of their present and prospective uses.

The value and price of a commodity rise or fall with demand, which will be, as before observed, according as the quantities of other commodities, including money, increase or diminish, while the quantity of this commodity remains unchanged.

If the quantity of money be increased, while the quantities of all other commodities remain stationary, more money must be given in exchange for each of them. In this case, the demand for money is reduced, while the demand for every other commodity is augmented. In other words, money is of less value, and all other commodities of greater.

If the quantity of wheat be increased, while that of all other commodities remains the same, more wheat must be given in exchange for each of them; that is, wheat is reduced both in value and price, while all other commodities are augmented in value, though not in price: for the proportion between the quantities of these and of money remains unchanged. If, in consequence of a short crop of grain throughout the country, the price of it should be doubled, the value of all other articles in relation to grain will be diminished one half; that is, twice as much of every thing must be given in exchange for grain. So far, the national wealth remains the same in value. What the consumer loses by the enhancement of the price, the producer gains. But should the nation import grain from abroad to supply the deficiency for necessary consumption, as much in amount as the quantity imported costs, so much in amount will the general wealth be reduced by the deficiency of the harvest.

In proportion to the aggregate increase of production may any single product be increased, without any diminution of its demand or its value.

And in proportion as products are multiplied and accumulated, so will the value of lands, buildings, and all other objects, of which the quantity is fixed or stationary, be increased.

Public measures, therefore, which by protecting industry lead to a multiplication of its products, and thereby to an augmentation of the general circulating capital, are measures which, in doing this, do as a consequence cause an augmentation of the income, and with that an increase of the value, of all real estate.

IV. DISTINCTION BETWEEN WEALTH AND VALUE.

Wealth is positive, value is relative. Wealth, as distinguished from value, consists in the positive quantities of material objects of necessity or desire, which have exchangeable value, or which possess utility conferred by labor, without exchangeable value. Value consists only in the relative quantities of things, and of those only which are objects of exchange.

If the quantities of all objects having exchangeable value be diminished in equal proportions, wealth, so far as it consists in these objects, would be diminished thereby in the average proportion; but the exchangeable value of each object would remain the same, and undiminished; for each object would still command the same quantity of every other object, that it did before the proportionate diminution.

The aggregate, however, of the diminished quantities of these objects would not support the same quantity of labor, or the same number of individuals as before; and in either circumstance the diminution of wealth plainly appears.

V. METALLIC MONEY.

Money is chiefly of gold and silver. It is in coin circulating by tale, or in mass circulating by weight.

It is introduced by foreign commerce, in exchange for the products of native industry.

It is one of the constituents of wealth, and is its universal representative. Like wealth, it gives its possessor, in all places within the sphere of civilization, a command of all objects of necessity or enjoyment, which are of an exchangeable nature. It is, by the common consent of nations, the medium through which one thing is exchanged for another, and the standard by which the relative values of things in exchange are measured.

Less money is required to facilitate the exchange of commodities, when their circulation is rapid, than when it is slow.

The variations in the value of money are caused by the greater or less demand there may be for it compared with the supply.

The value of money is greater, in proportion as the actual supply is less than the present demand; and its value is less, in proportion as the actual supply of it is greater than the present demand.

The increase of money, if it be employed to promote industry, is beneficial; it increases property. But if it merely beget speculation and augment expenditure, it is injurious; it diminishes property.

The interest of money, while it is held on hand, being lost, people will not hold a greater quantity by them, than what their occasions require. More than this, therefore, will not be retained in circulation; and any surplus, which may arise, will from time to time go off to the public benefit by its employment in foreign commerce.

To prohibit by law the exportation of money, increases its value in relation to the products of the country, which prohibits it; and diminishes its value in relation to all imported commodities. In other words, it causes native products to fall in price, and foreign commodities to rise in price.

The foreign commodities will rise in price, in consequence of the hazard and expense incurred in getting out of the country the money which may be given in payment for them; and the native products will fall, in consequence of the increasing scarcity of money caused by its constant departure; for in spite of the law to prevent it, it will find its way out, to seek for more profitable employment in countries where it has more extensive uses, and from which it will not be likely to return again.

Money will never leave countries, where its employment is free and unlimited, to take up its abode in those, where its movements are limited, and its employment restricted.

The effect of this prohibition, therefore, seems to be to produce a scarcity of money, to lower the price of native products, and as a consequence of this, to check the progress of industry and wealth.

VI. BANK CURRENCY.

Bank paper is used as a substitute for metallic money. It carries with it a bank-promise to pay on demand the sum of money which it represents; and while this promise is observed with good faith, it performs all the functions of metallic currency.

Banks issue their notes by loans on interest; and as the more they issue the greater their profit, they are tempted to loan out more than circulation can retain. They soon learn, however, by experience, what quantity they can keep out without its return for specie. But if, nevertheless, greedy of gain, they issue more than they can redeem, aud suspend payment, they commit a deliberate fraud upon the holders of their paper, to the amount of the depreciation which will consequently take place.

Legislative checks to banks discounting on their own stocks render them more safe, as well to a portion of the stockholders as to the community at large, and tend to prevent their unnecessary multiplication.

Most of the losses, which the public have sustained from bank failures, have been owing to the means, which discounting on their own stocks have afforded to speculating individuals to obtain their direction.

And the needless multiplication of banks is also owing to the facility, with which, by this kind of discount, they can be got up, with the advance of little or no capital.

The increase of banks of issue, when the supply of their paper is already equal to the demand, is a loss to the community, in as far as it is an increase of expenditure, without any increase of utility.

The banks cannot togetner force into circulation over a limited amount of their bills ; and for this reason, that, as there is a loss of interest on all money kept on hand, people will not keep more by them than their immediate occasions require, and the surplus there may be will consequently be returned to the banks for specie.

When one bank forces more than its proportion of bills into circulation, it is by crowding out in the same proportion the bills of other banks.

When a bank at one place is established with the capital of another place, the money, as it is loaned out, goes off in exchange for commodities which come in, or for things already there, but owned or owed for elsewhere; and, after a short period, the amount retained in circulation will be about the same as it was before.

In as far as the multiplication of banks has a tendency to increase expenditure, without in a corresponding degree increasing industry, it leads to great embarrassment, as has been the case throughout the interior of the Union.

When banks, however, are controlled by judicious checks, the use of their paper is a saving to the community, to the amount of the interest of the metallic money, which it releases from circulation, and which, being then set at liberty, goes to increase the capital employed in foreign commerce.

VII. INTEREST.

The rate of interest is regulated by the demand there is for money; and the demand in a great measure depends upon the profit on the employment of capital.

The demand for money, however, is occasionally augmented by the want of it for the payment of debts, and the supply of consumption, whereby the rate of interest is for a time enhanced.

In proportion as the general circulating capital, of which money is a component part, increases, the profit on the employment of it diminishes; and as the profit on the employment of capital diminishes, the rate of interest diminishes. Therefore the permanent abundance or scarcity of money only lowers or raises the rate of interest, in proportion as its presence or its absence augments or reduces the quantity of the general circulating capital.

Whatever is paid for the use of money beyond the market-rate of interest, is paid as a premium to the lender to compensate him for the risk he runs, of not being repaid without expense and delay, or of losing his money altogether.

Laws limiting the rate of interest on loans, diminish competition among lenders, and raise the rate of interest in the market. The borrower, besides being obliged to pay this higher rate of interest, is also obliged to pay to the lender such an additional sum, as will cover the risk which the lender runs, of losing his money by infringing the law.

Thus it seems that usury-laws, instead of favoring and protecting those for whose benefit they were intended, namely, the needy, do, on the contrary, actually compel them to incur a much heavier debt to obtain the means of succor, than they would otherwise be required to do.

It is not only, however, as these laws aggravate the evil they were intended to correct, that their expediency is to be objected to, but upon other grounds they are still more objectionable.

They tend to diminish the force of moral obligation. They invite to acts of dishonor, baseness, and fraud; and this by offering a discharge from debt as their reward. And thus they lead the unfortunate debtor from pecuniary embarrassment, to a state of moral degradation.

Further, when the profit on the employment of capital raises the market-rate of interest above the rate limited by law, it compels, in the transaction of business, to a very general evasion of the law. And in this respect, it is a question for legislators to determine, whether it be good policy to enact or retain laws of this nature, which, by accustoming the people to violations of law, tend to impair the respect wherein the laws generally ought to be held.

It is moreover a question, whether, instead of endeavoring to prevent the idle, the improvident, and the prodigal, by these laws, from parting with property which they know not how to use, it would not be better for society to leave them at liberty to transfer it to other hands, where it would be used productively to the public benefit.

This change of property, while it would promote the interest of the community on the one hand, might prove, to those who parted with it, a profitable lesson of experience on the other. It would lead them, through necessity, to a knowledge of the advantages of industry, providence, and economy; and with this knowledge, they would not be likely to require the interposition of usury-laws for their protection.

These, as well as all other legislative enactments, which interpose obstacles to the punctual performance of ordinary contracts, entered into in prosecution of the common affairs of life, have the effect to produce distrust, diminish confidence, abridge credit, discourage industry, and therewith to retard the progress of public prosperity and wealth.

VIII. PRODUCTION, USE, AND CONSUMPTION.

The results of production are products. Products are not *consumed*, while *in use;* they are consumed only when *by* use they are *annihilated.*

Wheat and wool are products. One is used for bread, and consumed in food; the other is used for cloth, and consumed in clothing.

Houses and household furniture are products. One is used for shelter, and the other is used for convenience.

The improvements of land are products, and used for profit or pleasure. In short, all things of a material nature, adapted by art and labor to consumption, use, or enjoyment, are products of industry and the results of production.

IX. PRODUCTIVE INDUSTRY.

Productive industry comprehends the exercise of talent, intelligence, invention, art, skill, dexterity, and labor, either in production, as in agriculture, the fisheries, manufactures, and the mechanic arts, or in the augmentation of the value of products, by the distribution and exchange of the transportable and circulating surplus, as in commerce.

The power of productive industry is measured by the quantities of its products in their relation to wealth, and not by their quantities in their relation to value; for the value of a product is increased by diminishing its relative quantity, whereas wealth is increased by the augmentation of the quantity of a product.

X. DISTINCTION BETWEEN PRODUCTIVE AND UNPRODUCTIVE LABOR.

It is not easy, in all cases, to draw a distinct line between productive and unproductive labor, nor is it of any practical importance that it should be done.

The following distinction may, however, be made between them. In private service, all labor, by which the exchangeable value of *material* objects is augmented, is productive labor; but that which adds nothing to the exchangeable value of material objects, notwithstanding it may be useful in other relations, is called unproductive labor.

In public service, all labor, which is employed to augment the utility of those objects, which come under the head of public property, is productive labor; whereas all other public labors, however important they may be to the public welfare, are nevertheless unproductive labors, in their relation to the production of wealth.

XI. OBJECTS OF PRODUCTION.

The objects of production are either perishable, and for immediate consumption; or more durable, and for present and future use and consumption. Those of the first kind are principally of agriculture and the fisheries; and those of the second, are mostly of manufacture and the mechanic arts. From the consumable products of this first department of industry, man principally derives his subsistence; in the more durable products of the second, he chiefly accumulates his wealth.

XII. DISTINCTION BETWEEN MANUFACTURE AND THE MECHANIC ARTS.

By the mechanic arts are understood the various arts, in which the operations are *manually* performed by the aid of tools and machines of little cost, and such as are within the means of the mechanic generally to procure for himself, without the aid of the capitalist.

By manufacture are understood those great productive operations of art, which cannot be effected without the assistance of large capitals: but by the employment of which, under the direction of skill, the powers of nature are brought through the medium of machinery to the aid of human labor, and made to perform its functions to such an extent, as greatly to augment production. And by means of this in the saving of labor, the costs of production are very considerably reduced, and the public supplied with the products, at a price reduced in a corresponding proportion.

XIII. PRODUCTIVE INDUSTRY, IN ITS RELATION TO THE PUBLIC WELFARE.

The more the national industry is diversified, and the more the number of its productive employments is multiplied, the greater is the demand for the products of labor in each employment.

This increases the profits of industry; the profits of industry increase the demand for labor; this raises the wages of labor, and the labor of the country is thereby more fully drawn into action.

Each successive new employment tends to increase the profits of existing employments. This it does in two ways; first, by diminishing competition in these employments; and, secondly, by furnishing additional consumers for their products. Thus, while the new employments augment the aggregate profits of the others, they diminish the number to participate in them, and cause thereby a much greater share of profit to go to each individual attached to them.

In this country, it is obvious that industry is not so productive, as it would become by being divided into a greater number of different employments. At present, about eight tenths of our population are attached to agriculture, while five tenths would probably produce an abundant supply for both the home and foreign demand for consumption, were there any profitable employment for the other three tenths.

The fact of so large a portion of our labor being unemployed, or only partially employed, tends to show that it would be promotive of national prosperity to encourage the production of every commodity, whatsoever it may be, which we possess as great natural advantages for producing, as the nations do from whom we now import the commodity. Any additional labor, which might be called into action by adequate encouragements to the establishment of new branches of industry, would, besides benefiting all the present branches, produce a gain for the nation to the whole value of their labor, be it more or less.

If we possess greater advantages than other nations, is it not better policy to endeavor to profit by them ourselves, than to give them up to foreign nations, that we may partake in the smaller advantages, which they have to offer in return?

Inequalities of condition arise among men, from the inequalities there are in their natural, physical, moral, and political advantages. The individual, however, who possesses superior advantages, let them arise from whatever cause they may, is, in conformity to the moral constitution of human nature, disposed to avail himself of them to the greatest extent he justly can. An individual, therefore, who with a view to gain, should cast all which constituted his superior advantages into a common stock, that he might share equally with those who contributed little or nothing, would be considered as destitute of common understanding.

So with respect to nations: some possess greater natural, moral, and political advantages than others. Now if the nation which possessed all these advantages in a greater degree than any other, should, under the influence of the visionary notion, that by each nation's making its peculiar advantages common to all, all would be gainers by it, give up its own superior advantages for the sake of sharing in the inferior ones of other nations, although in so doing it might imagine itself pursuing a very liberal policy, yet it would deserve the reproach of acting with a total ignorance of its own interests.

Industry contributes to the happiness of man in two ways: first, by the gratifications, which the possession, use, and consumption of its products afford him; and secondly, by the useful occupations, professions, and pursuits, to which the desire to possess these gratifications leads him. And his happiness, perhaps, depends as much upon the latter as the former: for he has generally as much pleasure in the pursuit of his object as he has in its attainment, and sometimes he has more. Indeed, at all times, a man is more happy while employed in the pursuit of some object, than he is while unemployed, and with no object of sufficient interest to pursue.

The more productive industry may become, by the aid of accumulating capital and machinery, which public encouragement may draw to it, the greater will be the facilities to the industrious for acquiring not only a comfortable living, but also riches. The greater, too, will be the number, at the same time, of those, whom it will release from the necessity of manual labor, to live by occupations and professions in which that is not required. And the greater, likewise, will be the number of those, whom it will release from all necessary occupations, and leave to that leisure, which may be employed in the cultivation of science and literature, and the diffusion of useful knowledge.

In those countries, where industry is seen to be associated with ignorance, poverty, and vice, it is owing to the oppressive and unequal operation of their political institutions.

But in this country, where the government proceeds from the people, where it is established upon the basis of their perfect equality, and is exercised by their representatives only for their welfare, we see that industry is connected with intelligence, property, and virtue, and that it offers, with these, the only security, upon which the continuance of the happy organization of our government depends.

XIV. CONFLICTING INTERESTS.

The conflicting interests of industry arise only from competition, and exist but among those of the same employments. There is no competition or conflict of interests between those of different occupations; they naturally promote each other's industry. None indeed can arise from differences in soil, or climate, or industry; these differences, on the contrary, harmonize interests.

The difference, even, in the means by which industry is prosecuted in the northern and southern states, is equally conducive to the wealth both of the one and of the other. The commerce and industry of the North increase with the prosperity of the South; and the industry of the South is aided and promoted in return by the capitals of the North; and the industry of the West by its intercourse with both. Connected as we are by the interchange of the products of our industry, the prosperity of one section contributes to the prosperity of the others; and the prosperity of one class, to that of all other classes.

Industry in one individual excites to industry in another, and the gain of wealth by one is employed to increase the gains of others. With the increase of wealth, expenditure is increased; and with expenditure, industry is promoted and wealth distributed.

Among ourselves, in the differences of our climate, our soil, and our employments, our interests are in unison; and the only interest which conflicts with any interest of ours, is that of foreign industry, which being more mature, competes with ours in its early efforts, to its discouragement. And as each division of our industry extends its benefits through every other division, the interests of the whole are promoted by government's extending to each its protection against the foreign competition in the home market.

The more industry is diversified, the more customers has each class for its products. The greatest stimulus, which can be given to any one kind of industry, is to excite to other kinds. This affords to each a greater market for its products, and a greater variety of articles in return for them.

XV. AGRICULTURE, IN RELATION TO THE GENERAL INTERESTS OF SOCIETY.

To enter upon agriculture in this country, very little capital, and as little skill are required. Wild land is cheap, and whoever can handle an axe, and is inured to labor, may soon possess a farm and support a family.

The facility with which a subsistence is thus procured, has induced the mass of our population to apply themselves to this occupation. The consequence is, that, for a time, throughout the interior, where every man is a farmer, and there is none to purchase his products, all are obliged to depend for the supply of their wants upon their household means.

Agriculture, in this state, contributes little to the augmentation of national wealth. But as population becomes denser, and other occupations and employments arise, it grows more productive, and in proportion as these multiply, so does the income of agriculture increase, and with its income its capital.

The greatest encouragement, which can be given to agriculture, is that which excites to other kinds of industry. This affords to the farmer a market for his produce, and such articles in return, as increase his enjoyments.

By the increase of other kinds of industry, the farmer not only has a better market for his produce, but he finds that it increases the value of his estate. By means of it, he at once has a better living and has become a richer man.

The establishment of new branches of industry tends to increase population, by the additional employment it affords to labor; and wherever we see population increasing from this cause, there we see also a rapid rise in the value of all real property.

Capital in agriculture yields a less income in proportion to its amount, than capital in either of the other branches of industry. The reason of this is, that the demand for agricultural capital is greater than for capital in other employments. That the demand is greater, arises from two circumstances; first, the greater security, which agriculture affords to the investment of capital; the second is, the greater number of persons there are, who, unskilled to get their living in other employments, seek it in employing themselves, with what property they may have, in agriculture. Thus, as there is greater competition and less skill in the employment of capital in agriculture than in the other branches of industry, the profits on its employment must necessarily be less in this than in the others.

In proportion as there is less skill employed in agriculture, than in the other productive branches, so must there be more labor employed to produce equal exchangeable values.

But though capital in proportion to its amount, and labor in proportion to its quantity, be less productive in agriculture than they are in other employments, yet, as the agricultural class is so much more numerous than the other classes, probably four times as numerous as all the others together, it is from this class that the greatest values towards the augmentation of the national wealth arise.

The rapid growth of the agricultural capital is owing to the operation of three causes. The first is, the large tracts of wild land, which are constantly coming under cultivation by the increase of population ; the second is, the constant rise in the value of lands under cultivation, owing to the increase of other branches of industry ; the third and last, is the addition annually made to the capital by what is saved from the annual product of agricultural industry.

Though agricultural industry becomes more productive as other kinds of industry increase, yet it will not possess its highest productive power, until the numbers of those in other occupations have so multiplied, as to create a demand for the produce of agriculture equal to the full power of its labor to supply.

XVI. MANUFACTURE, IN RELATION TO THE GENERAL INTERESTS OF SOCIETY.

Manufacture, operating by the powers of nature through the means of machinery and skill, is a branch of industry, which does not arise out of the necessities of man, neither does it necessarily grow up from his abundance.

It is only through public encouragement and protection, that it can be introduced into a country.

Before it can be established, capital must have been accumulated, and a competent degree of skill acquired. These are seldom united in the same person. One person possesses the capital and another the skill; and without their co operation its establishment cannot take place. No person will endanger his capital in a new enterprise, without a prospect of profit, which more than counterbalances the hazard of loss.

Their co-operation, therefore, to this end, cannot be brought about without public regulations, which alone can afford that prospect of safety and profit, which induces to the undertaking.

It is only by the regulations which impose duties on the importation of foreign manufacture, that the inducements are afforded to the employment of capital and skill in the establishment of domestic manufacture.

But although capital and skill and a protecting duty are pre-requisites to the establishment of manufacture; yet it is only while the new establishments are forming, maturing, and perfecting their skill and machinery, that protecting duties will be required.

The first effect of the introduction of manufacture is to produce a great augmentation of the public wealth, by the additional value which it immediately imparts to all real estate, within a marketable distance of its establishments.

And then, through the labor employed in forming the establishments, a great amount of capital is put in circulation, which, in passing from hand to hand, produces increased activity in every department of industry.

Villages, schools, and churches arise around the manufactory, by the means it affords for their erection and support.

The farmer has a better market, the mechanic more employment, the laborer higher wages, and those of other useful vocations a greater income.

And, unless the labor employed in forming the establishments be taken from other branches of industry to the diminution of their products, the whole value produced by it is, to the amount of it, so much clear gain to the country.

But the labor, heretofore employed for that purpose, has not been to diminish, but to increase, production in other branches. For to increase the number of laborers in one employment does not reduce production in others, except when the whole productive labor of a country is fully employed. But this is not the case with us. We have more labor than can be profitably employed.

If the new establishments afford to the employment of capital a greater profit, and to labor higher wages, than their employment in other branches of industry affords, they will attract surplus capital and labor from the other branches. This, by increasing competition in the new establishments, gradually lowers the profits of their capital, and the wages of the labor which they employ; while at the same time, by diminishing competition in the other branches, it raises the profits of the capital, and the wages of the labor which these employ.

And thus, as the profits of capital and the wages of labor are lowered in the one, so they are raised in the others, till they both, in all employments, come to a new level, but to a higher one than that at which they stood before.

The advantages, flowing from the establishment of manufactories, are not, however, confined to the section of country in which they may happen to be situated, but are extended through the intervention of commerce over the Union.

The planter shares them, for example. His interest is promoted by the increased consumption which the domestic manufacture produces, of his great staple, cotton. He is also benefited by the manufactured products being supplied to him in return, at a cheaper rate than they would have been, if public encouragement had not established manufacture among us.

All others are benefited in like manner, if not in the same degree.

Manufacture, in the multiplication of its products, increases the demand for the products of the other branches of industry, in so much as there is more produced to be given in exchange for those other products.

The industry of the nation is productive, in proportion to the capital and skill employed through the medium of machinery in aid of labor to accelerate production ; and not in proportion to the number of its laborers. It is in manufacture, that capital and skill are employed in the greatest degree, in proportion to labor ; and it is there, that, by their means, labor is rendered more productive than it is in any other employment.

The products of the labor of a few hands in manufacture will purchase the products of many hands in agriculture.

Manufacture has, in this country, already so multiplied its products, as to supply commerce, both inland and foreign, with considerable additional employment in their distribution.

It has also added considerably to our exports, by which the imports are increased, and the public revenue augmented.

XVII. THE MECHANIC ARTS, IN RELATION TO THE GENERAL INTERESTS OF SOCIETY.

The mechanic arts comprehend all the divisions of manual labor, in which art, skill, and dexterity are employed to modify and compound matter, materials, and rude products, and to adapt them to the consumption, use, and gratification of man.

The individuals employed in these arts form a numerous class in society, and compose the most considerable portion of the population of towns and cities.

It is through the general consumption and the labors of this class, chiefly, that the perishable and consumable surplus of agriculture is converted into fixed and durable property.

In the mechanic arts, it is not so much by the employment of capital, which merely supplies the tools to work with and the materials to work upon, as it is by the diligence, skill, and dexterity, with which labor is prosecuted, directed, and applied to its various objects, that the industry of this class, in proportion to its magnitude, is more productive than the industry of the agricultural.

XVIII. COMMERCE, IN RELATION TO THE GENERAL INTERESTS OF SOCIETY.

Nature having made mankind dependant one upon another for the supply of their mutual wants, the interchange of the products of their labor to this end was a thing of necessity. From this necessity commerce had its origin, and with its progress civilization advanced, industry increased, and the comforts and enjoyments of life were multiplied.

Commerce, by the means which it affords to industry for the exchange of its products, enables this, in all situations, to direct its operations to that object, which yields the greatest return, and to the production of such articles as are most peculiarly adapted to soil and climate.

Commerce encourages industry, and industry in return supports commerce; they act and react upon each other to their mutual advantage. The more industry multiplies its products, the more employment there is for commerce in their distribution. The greater the diversity of employments in a community, the greater is its industry; and the more industry is subdivided the more productive it becomes. But it is by the employment of natural powers in aid of human labor, and by means of machinery, that production is most rapidly accelerated; and it is therefore by those public measures, which lead to these productive results, that commerce is most to be encouraged.

An apprehension, however, prevails, though without just cause, that the encouragement of domestic manufacture by duties on the import of foreign manufacture, would restrict and curtail foreign commerce. The effect is directly the reverse. The measure increases internal industry, and with the increase of that, foreign commerce increases. There is not an article of our exports, which we should export the less of, in consequence of our importing less of foreign manufactures, excepting, perhaps, that portion of cotton, which, if we did not manufacture it ourselves, would have entered into the manufacture of the foreign cotton goods, which we should have imported. But, even in respect to that, commerce is a great gainer by the measure in question; since the employment, for both navigation and capital, in transporting the cotton for a given quantity of goods from the southern states for manufacture in the more northern, is more than double what there would have been in transporting to Europe that portion of our cotton, which would have entered into the manufacture of an equal quantity of goods there. And our commerce having the exclusive supply of this material for the home manufacture, but less than half the supply of it for the foreign, will gain twice as much by supplying the increasing use of it at home, as it will lose by any diminished use of it from that cause abroad.

Our exports are of the sea, the forest, mechanic arts, agriculture, and of manufacture; and what article is there, which comes under these heads, that any nation will require the less of, because we require less of British manufacture? Not one, with the previous exception of cotton. Our exports then will continue undiminished, and the net proceeds of them will be invested in foreign products; and though some of the objects of investment will be changed, the amount of investment will be undiminished.

Of our foreign commerce, that is most to our advantage, which is with people, whose climate and industry are different from ours, and who take from us, for their consumption, the products natural to our climate and industry, and give us in exchange therefor other products, peculiar to their climate and industry.

Such is the commerce of our northern states with the West

and East Indies, South America, Africa, and the Atlantic Islands; and of our southern States with Europe. In this trade, our industry is encouraged by the peculiar returns it gets for its reward. Of these returns, after our own wants are supplied, a large surplus remains, in which consist the profits of the trade. With that portion of this surplus, which results from the commerce of the northern states with the East and West Indies, and so forth, we now enter into another branch of our foreign commerce, which is with nations, whose climate and industry are similar to ours, namely, the nations of Europe.

In this branch of commerce, we, in a great measure, expend the profits gained in the former branch, and we do it to our disadvantage in the purchase of various manufactures, most of which, were if not for the discouragement which the importation of them thus produces, would be furnished by our own industry. And when this industry is sufficiently encouraged, that surplus will then be employed to import other articles which our wants will require, instead of manufactures; but which, until that be the case, we must forego the use of, for want of the means of making the purchase.

The additions to public wealth, from commerce, are made up of the profits gained by the parties on both sides, in the exchange of commodities. The farmer, when he exchanges his beef, pork, and flour with the merchant for tea, coffee, and sugar, and consumes them, adds nothing to his property, although he does to his enjoyments. But when he exchanges them for money, and with that employs the builder, carpenter, and joiner to enlarge his accommodations and multiply his conveniences, he not only adds to his comforts, but he increases his wealth, and at the same time imparts benefits to the persons whom he employs.

The merchant, on his part, exports his beef, pork, and flour, and receives from abroad a greater quantity of tea, coffee, sugar, and money in exchange for them, than he gave the farmer. Of this additional quantity, that, which remains after paying the expenses incurred in the operation, is the profit or product of his capital and industry, and is, to the amount of it, so much added to his general capital. And he, by repeating this operation, with means each time increased, continues to add more and more to his capital, till he finds that, as this is augmented, the profits on its employment are diminished. Now, therefore, he is induced, with a view to greater profit, to give a portion of it another direction. This he does by employing it in the purchase of mill-sites, the erection of buildings, the construction of machinery, the establishment of manufactories; by doing which he not only increases his own wealth, but adds to that of the community.

For in this country, in the present state of its industry, as agricultural production exceeds the home and foreign consumption together, every additional employment of labor in other occupations may be considered, to the value of the products of it, so much clear gain to the nation, or in other words, so much more gained than would have been gained, had not the labor been thus employed.

Navigation not only affords one of the most productive sources of the increase of public wealth, but it also supplies powerful means to be employed in public defence. It rears up a class of patriotic, hardy, and daring men, always ready for the public service when called for; and it is no small advantage to the nation to have constantly at command so efficient a force, free of any expense to support it.

Notwithstanding, however, the importance of navigation to the public prosperity and security, that portion of it, which is employed in foreign commerce, is the only one of all the divisions of industry, which receives no compensation for what it contributes towards the protection of the industry of others against foreign competition.

When the husbandman pays more, in consequence of the duty on imports, to the home manufacturer for the cloth bought of him, the husbandman gets as much more in return, from the same cause, for the wool which he sells the manufacturer, and thus the thing is equalized between them. But it is not so with the ship-owner in foreign trade. Though he pays more for the materials which enter into the construction of his ship, in consequence of the duties laid on the importation to encourage the home production, he gets no return for it. He cannot, on that account, add any thing to the rate of freight, because he, being in open competition with the foreign ship-owner, must carry as low as he does, or else remain unemployed.

Therefore, were a drawback allowed on ship-building, at so much per ton, to the amount of the duties on the foreign materials used in their construction, it would, in respect to the general system of encouragement, be no more than plaçing this branch of industry upon a just equality with the others, and we should then be able with our ships to enter into competition against foreign shipping upon more equal terms. The effect of doing this, hôwever, would be rather to increase ship-building than to give profit to ship-owners; for the increase of ships would, by competition, reduce the rate of freight, and lower the profit of ship-owners to about the same level it was at before. But every other individual, who produced an article for export, or consumed an article of import, would, in the reduction of freight, be a gainer; for every diminution of expense in the transportation of an article increases the consumption of it, by lowering its price to the consumer.

That portion of navigation, which is employed in the coasting trade, is of more consequence than that employed in the foreign. Its tonnage is greater, and is rapidly increasing with the increasing industry of the country. Like the navigation in foreign trade, it is productive of wealth by the value which it adds to commodities by their transport; and it is so in an equal degree with that. For when one employment of vessels is more profitable than the other, vessels are turned from one to the other employment, until the profit is equalized between them.

Navigation in the coasting trade, in respect to its influence in exciting to production in the different divisions of industry, operates with double the effect that our navigation in foreign trade does, because our foreign navigation divides its influence, employing one half of it at home to the encouragement of home industry, and carrying the other half abroad to the equal encouragement of foreign industry. Whereas the coastwise navigation, though it divides it influence between the places it connects in intercourse, yet employs the whole of it at home, to the encouragement of home production.

Our inland and coastwise trade is beyond comparison more important to national interests than our foreign commerce. It employs more tons of navigation than the foreign ; and the vessels it employs make several interchanges of merchandise, while the vessels employed in the foreign trade are making but one. It employs more capital, in proportion as the amount of goods to be exchanged by it is greater; and the capital employed affords equal profit in proportion to its amount. The home market for the surplus products of our various industry, with the exception of two or three articles of southern produce, is probably of four times the extent of the foreign market.

The interchange of domestic products among ourselves excites our interest doubly as much as does the interchange of products between us and foreign nations. When commerce exchanges the cotton of the southern states for the productions of the northern, it promotes equally the industry of both. But when commerce exchanges it with foreign nations for their cotton goods, it encourages industry in only one section of the Union, discourages it in another, and promotes it abroad. And by our consumption of the foreign cotton goods with which our foreign commerce thus supplies us, the cotton planter of the southern states is only about half as much encouraged in the cultivation of cotton, as he would be by our consumption of an equal quantity of cotton goods of home manufacture. For the home manufacturer uses none but cotton of domestic cultivation; whereas the foreign manufacturers use about as much cotton produced in other countries, as they do of cotton of this country, in the manufacture of their goods. Therefore, in consuming foreign cotton goods, we encourage the culture of cotton in foreign countries as much as in our own.

Our political institutions facilitate, to talents and industry engaged in useful pursuits, the acquisition of wealth; but at the same time guard against the pernicious effects of a too great inequality in its possession, by requiring its distribution in the course of descent. Thus, while they prevent the withdrawing of any portion of the national wealth for the perpetual aggrandizement of a few families to the impoverishment of many, they provide that the whole property of the nation, real as well as personal, without reserve, shall be placed within the reach of all, as a common fund, out of which productive industry and the exercise of useful talents may draw their full reward.

In the excitement to active industry, and to the exercise of talents, thus produced by our political institutions,—in the extent of our territory,—in the variety of our soils and climates and labors,—in our uncontrolled choice of pursuit, and unrestricted freedom of intercourse,—in all this, our home commerce possesses advantages, by means of which, with the public regulations which protect it against foreign interposition, and with the increase of population and industry, it is destined to attain a greater magnitude and higher degree of prosperity, than the home commerce of any other nation has ever attained.

XIX. COTTON CULTURE.

The cotton culture is a very productive and rapidly increasing branch of agricultural industry. It furnishes a material for manufacture, which, beside supplying the home demand, constitutes a third or more of our whole domestic export. It employs a large portion of our navigation, foreign and coast-wise, in its transportation, and gives extensive employment to commercial capital and agency. The increasing demand for it is owing mostly to the great improvements made in the machinery employed in its manufacture, which, by enabling the goods to be sold at so cheap a rate, has greatly increased their consumption, and caused them to supersede in many instances the use of linen and woollen.

The foreign manufacturer, as mentioned in a previous article, works up the cotton of all other nations, whereas the home manufacturer works up only that of domestic growth. The reason of this difference is, that the home market is secured to the home cultivator, by a protecting duty sufficient to exclude foreign cottons. Otherwise our manufacturers would find it as much for their interest to use the cottons produced in foreign countries, as the foreign manufacturer finds it for his, and they would be imported accordingly. But as the home market is also secured, or nearly secured, by the same means to the home manufacturer, there is a reciprocity of advantage in contributing to each other's protection against foreign competition. As the home manufacturer uses double the quantity of cotton of our growth, that the foreign manufacturer does in making the same quantity of goods, the increase of the home manufacture affords double the encouragement to the home cultivator, that the same increase in the foreign manufacture would afford. In consuming cotton goods of foreign manufacture, we encourage the cultivator of foreign cotton, as much as we do our own; whereas in consuming cotton goods of domestic manufacture we encourage only our own culture. The domestic cotton goods are now articles of considerable exportation; and as they are wholly of our cotton, while foreign cotton goods are made of cotton whereof ours composes but half, the more our goods supplant the foreign in other foreign markets, the more will our culture of cotton be promoted.

XX. INTERNAL IMPROVEMENT.

Internal improvement, made to facilitate intercourse, operates through all the various interests of society, in the augmentation of national wealth. In its primary operation, it removes obstructions to the interchange of commodities, and causes labor and capital to be turned from transportation to be employed in production. In reducing the expenses of transportation, it increases national industry, and renders it more productive of both quantity and value in all its branches. By the removal of obstructions to intercourse, it brings the various branches of industry nearer to each other; and the nearer they are brought, the more they promote each other's interests, and the interests of the whole community; for the nearer they are, the more is saved in transport between them; and what is saved in transport is so much gained, and equally shared between producer and consumer. It raises the value of lands within the sphere of its influence, in proportion as it increases the value of their produce. It augments the circulating capital to the amount of the additional quantity of produce, which through its means becomes an object of transport. It increases the products of agricultural industry, and it increases the products of other branches of industry to be exchanged for them. It increases commerce by increasing the quantity of products to be transported and distributed by it. And though internal improvement is thus operative in the promotion of industry and the general increase of wealth, the work itself, in which the improvement consists, is executed without the reduction of capital.

The money employed for the payment of labor merely changes hands, and remains in the community to the same amount it would have done, had not the labor been so employed; and as for the necessary consumption of the laborer, that is the same that it would have been had he been idle. The labor employed in this way is not to the diminution of production in any branch of industry. It is chiefly taken from the surplus hands attached to agriculture. It estimated that one third of the population of a country engaged in agriculture can produce enough for the consumption of the whole. In this country more than eight tenths belong to this class, whereas less than half of our population could produce an abundant supply both for home and foreign consumption. Therefore, to employ the surplus hands in other occupations, or in works of public or private utility, would be a gain to the community to the whole amount of the value of their labor.

XXI. DUTIES ON IMPORTS.

Of the public revenue, that portion, which is raised by duties on the importation of foreign commodities, is raised in a manner most consistent with the general welfare. It is paid by the consumer in the price of the commodity; and whether he buys it or not is a matter of choice with him, and not of necessity; for every thing of necessity may be produced among ourselves.

Of the duties on the importation of foreign commodities, those, which are imposed upon such commodities, as, with the acquisition of skill and dexterity, we can produce with as little labor at home, as they are produced with abroad, are the kind of duties, which, while they contribute to the public revenue, operate at the same time most to the encouragement of the public industry.

A high duty on particular commodities to promote the home production of them, although it diminishes their importation, yet as other commodities take their place, it does not diminish the general amount of imports.

The imports are always equal to the net proceeds of the exports, and the exports are equal to the foreign demand.

The foreign demand is regulated by the foreign want for consumption; and this is not affected by the fact of whether we consume more or less of foreign manufactures.

Therefore, as the diminished importation of particular commodities only changes the objects of investment abroad, a high duty for the encouragement of home manufacture has no tendency to diminish the public revenue, but on the contrary to augment it, by the additions which the manufacture, in its progress, causes to be made to the exports.

For while we continue to export the same staples to the same extent as before, the new branches of industry, arising from the encouragement which the duties afford, furnish other products in addition to the old ones to be exported, by which in return the amount of imports, and consequently the public revenue, are augmented.

Although, by the effect of the increase of duties, which causes home products to supplant foreign products in the home market, the price of them to the consumer is in the first instance enhanced; yet this causes such a competition among the home producers, that the price of them to the consumer is soon reduced below what it was before the duties were increased; and the permanent reduction a great deal more than compensates him for the temporary enhancement.

The new branches of industry, to which the increase of duties gives rise, leads to an increased production in all existing branches. For, by the products of the new branches, the quantity of circulating capital is augmented; and as much as the products of the new branches add to its quantity, so much more will there be to be given in exchange for the products of existing branches, and the demand for these products will be in that proportion greater.

However low the wages of labor may be in foreign countries, and however cheap we may import commodities from them in consequence of it, nevertheless it would be injurious to the interest of the nation, to import any such commodities, as the nation possesses natural advantages for producing within itself, equal to those possessed by the foreign countries from which they might be imported.

If it were for our interest to import any such commodity, merely because the cost by importation would be less than the cost by home production, it would be still more for our interest, for the same reason, to import it if we could to cost nothing. To be sure it would, will it be said.—But let us see if that would be the case.

Suppose, for instance, we were to import a sufficiency of wheat, free of cost, for the supply of all those, who now depend for their supply upon the surplus of our own agriculture. The consequence would be that the farmer, no longer able to sell his wheat, would suffer the privation of all those comforts and enjoyments, which it before procured for him. But the farmer would not be the only person to suffer. The manufacturer, the mechanic, and the merchant would feel its effects. They depend more upon the agricultural class for employment and business, than upon all the other classes together; and this class being no longer able to sell the chief products of its industry, would be disabled from contributing towards the support of the other classes, by the purchase of the products of their industry. Thus general embarrassment and distress would be extended, by such importation, through all the divisions of industry in the community.

If therefore, as it appears in this case, it would not be for our advantage to import any such article as we produce among ourselves, even though it cost us nothing, it surely could not be for our advantage to import such articles, merely because it came a little cheaper by importation than by home production.

We will now take another article, not necessary to subsistence, like wheat, but only to comfort, shoes, for example, and suppose them, like wheat, to be imported free of cost. The consequence would be that the whole class, who support themselves by the production of that article would be thrown out of employment, and the community would lose more by the loss of that branch of productive industry, than they would gain by having their shoes for nothing.

If any one imagines that the individuals of this class, thus thrown out of employment, may employ themselves in the other branches of industry, and that their labor in these other branches would be equally productive to the nation, he lies under a great mistake.

By having this class enter into them, these other branches of industry would find the demand for their products diminished. They would lose the demand for that portion of their products, which this class before took up as consumers. This would cause a diminution of their profits. And their profits would not only be reduced by the loss of this class as consumers; but they would be still further reduced by having these consumers converted into producers, which would cause the reduced profits to be divided among a greater number.

There is no existing branch of industry, which does not, without such accession, already supply a greater quantity of its products than is demanded for consumption. When this is the case, no additional production would take place in consequence of such accession to the numbers of those before employed; and the only effect of it would be, therefore, to diminish profits and relax industry.

From this case it is clear, as in the former case of wheat, that we can be no gainers by the importation of any commodity, which we can produce with as little labor at home as its production requires abroad, however cheap it may come, even though it come for nothing.

It would be for our interest that no commodity should be imported, which we possess within ourselves natural advantages for producing, equal to those of the country from which the commodity is imported, while we are only deficient in a certain degree of skill, which with suitable encouragement we should soon acquire, and which, when acquired, would enable us to produce with as little labor as the foreign country. In producing these commodities at home, a saving to the whole amount of the expenses of the foreign importation would ultimately result to the consumer, and a gain to the nation of the sum total of the value of the commodities produced.

It is no good argument against the encouragement of home production, that the wages of labor are lower in foreign countries than in our own, and that therefore it would be cheaper to import, unless it were for the general welfare that the laboring classes in the country, who compose the mass of the nation, should be reduced to the same degraded condition, in which they are in some of the states of Europe. And for this surely none will contend.

In this country, where subsistence is cheap and easily procured, it requires the stimulus of high wages to call labor into action.

And it is only by measures, which render productive industry more profitable, by securing to it the supply of the home market, that the demand for labor is increased. This raises the wages, and calls a greater quantity into employment; and the greater the quantity of labor employed, the more rapid will be the production of wealth; and the higher the wages the more equal will be the distribution of wealth.

By the importation of foreign commodities, such as our soil, climate, and industry are adapted to produce, and such as we should produce if we did not import them, national industry is discouraged and the progress of wealth retarded.

But by the importation of all such commodities, as our soil, climate, and industry are not adapted to produce, national industry is encouraged, and the progress of wealth accelerated.

By the importation of teas, coffee, silks, and other luxuries, wealth is promoted in two ways. First, by the luxuries being placed within reach, a desire is excited to possess them, which stimulates to the additional labor, necessary for obtaining them; and in the products of this labor given in exchange for them, a profit is realized, which is so much added to the commercial capital. Secondly, the additional labors, to which the desire of obtaining these luxuries stimulates, contributes to the formation of those habits of industry, which commonly have for their ultimate object that accumulation, upon which depends the general increase of wealth.

The capital of a nation arises from the employment of its labor, and however much the political institutions of a country may favor the equal distribution of property, capital will accumulate in some hands, while it will not in others. Thus one portion of the community will possess the capital, and another will perform the labor.

Now it would be highly for the benefit of the whole, to have such a state of things exist, that they, who possess the capital, should find it more to their profit to employ with it the labor of their own country, than to employ with it the labor of foreign countries. For then our capital, instead of going to foreign countries for the support of labor there, would remain at home to encourage, employ, and support our own labor, that labor, from which alone our whole wealth is derived.

But as the degraded labor of some of the European states is cheaper than the labor of this country, our capital will go off to the support of this foreign labor, unless the government, by the adequate protection of national industry, renders it more advantageous for the possessors of capital to employ and support labor with it at home.

The high wages of labor in this country are nearly connected with the permanence of our political institutions and the progress of the general welfare. Upon high wages depend the more equal distribution of property, the means of more general education, and the more extensive diffusion of useful knowledge. And the support of these wages will mainly depend upon the degree of protection, which government may afford, to the various pursuits of national industry.

XXII. EXCHANGE ON ENGLAND.

In our foreign commerce, Great Britain takes from us only certain commodities, the produce of our soil, and such only as she cannot produce from her own. We take from her all kinds of commodities, whether of her soil or of her manufacture, and such as we might produce from our own industry. Of these, we take from her to the amount of several millions of dollars more than the products amount to, which she takes from us.

The nations of the continent of Europe take from us not only the kinds of commodities which Great Britain takes, but they also take other commodities, the surplus of our imports from the West and East Indies, South America, and Africa, to the amount of several millions of dollars more than what we take from them is worth. This balance in our favor, of several millions of dollars, from our trade with these nations, we receive in money from them, which we remit to Great Britain to pay her the balance against us, of several millions ofdollars, arising out of trade with her. This money, together with the proceeds of our exports to Great Britain, is there placed to the credit of the American exporter.

The American exporter thus has money in England, which he wants to employ in this country. On the other hand, the American importer of English goods has money in this country, which he wants to employ in England. Now if the want between these should be equal, of the exporter who has his money abroad to use it at home, and of the importer who has his money at home to use it abroad, as many dollars will be given in America for a bill in pounds sterling on England, as that bill will purchase of dollars in England. The *value* of exchange will vary a little from this, according as the want on one side or the other may be more or less, to have money at home which is abroad, or to have money abroad which is at home; but it cannot vary to exceed the cost of transporting the money, which, in a state of peace, including insurance, is less than two per cent.

The reason that the *rate* of exchange on England is at times so much above par, is, that the pound sterling in England will purchase more dollars there at such times, than what we estimate the par value of it in dollars to be in America.

The great differences in the rate of exchange on England beyond the expense of transporting specie, which from time to time arise, are caused, by the fluctuations in the value of British currency. The pound sterling will not, in Great Britain, purchase two thirds of the gold or silver or British goods at one time, which it will at another time. It is by the quantity of gold or silver, which the pound sterling will purchase in Great Britain, and by taking into calculation the expense of transporting gold or silver either way, according as the demand for money may be, that we determine the value in dollars of a bill of exchange in pounds sterling on England.

OBSERVATIONS

ON

SMITH'S WEALTH OF NATIONS.

---

1. The Inquiry into the Nature and Causes of the Wealth of Nations, by Adam Smith, was first published in 1776. The same doctrines were taught by him, and substantially the same matter disclosed to his pupils, upwards of twenty years before that, in his lectures as professor in the university of Glasgow. But, out of Scotland, little was known of his views until they were printed; and the revolution occasioned by them in the science of political economy, is dated in that period, ever memorable to Americans. The novelty and boldness of the opinions inculcated in Smith's Wealth of Nations, the easy, natural, and expressive style of his composition, the many important truths he disclosed, the lucid explanations he gave of many points previously deemed obscure and difficult, the general ignorance of the people concerning the subjects considered by him, all these circumstances conspired to give his work a speedy and extensive celebrity.—Things, about which, notwithstanding their intrinsic importance, comparatively few persons had thought at all, fewer thought correctly or understandingly, and very few written to any useful purpose, began to become the topic of familiar discourse and of constant discussion in every shape.—Somewhat, it is true, had been published on the nature of public wealth in England,

France, and elsewhere, and most of all perhaps in Italy, who, as she gained the start of other modern European nations in the cultivation of the useful as well as the liberal arts, so also she produced some of the most early and intelligent authors on political economy.—But common consent of writers at the present day seems to attribute the consequence, if not of the whole science of political economy, yet of the prevailing doctrines of the science, to the writings of Adam Smith.

There is no doubt of the merits of this philosopher. While it is impossible for all to accede to the fundamental principle, or to a number of the separate doctrines, either of his theory of Moral Sentiments, or of his Inquiry concerning the Wealth of Nations, it is alike impossible to be insensible to the beauty and value, in many respects, of each of these publications.—Indeed, the importance of his economical views is manifested not more by the multitude of his disciples, than by the multitude of those, who stand in opposition to him. It is great evidence of an author's merit that he is believed by a numerous body of men; but it is hardly less evidence of the same thing, that many have combated, or attempted to confute, his reasonings and opinions.

In the following remarks, the writer's aim has been briefly to expose the fallacy, not of every thing in the Inquiry, which is open to exception; but chiefly of doctrines, which, he conceives, are of tendency injurious to the welfare of his country. Adam Smith has founded a *school* in political economy, who, like the school of Quesnay and his fellow economists in France, are too plausible in the defence and too zealous in the advancement of their favorite theory, not to have gained a host of proselytes. What influence they may obtain abroad, is of little consequence to us; or certain it is, rather, that the more influence they do exert in Europe, the better they will promote the interests of America. But it is time for us to be vigilant and circumspect, when men and men of letters among us, who deservedly possess great credit in the public mind, profess themselves emulous to pin their faith on the infallibility of Adam Smith. When this becomes apparent, it is evidently time to exhibit the proofs of his fallibility, and of the pernicious effects arising from injudicious application of his theories to practice.

It is not singular to question the soundness of many of Smith's doctrines. Even his disciples, his warmest admirers, admit that the Inquiry is extremely defective in arrangement; that there is a want of precision and certainty in some of the most important parts of his book; that he is not always consistent with himself or with fact; that his work is without any pretensions to the rank of a complete and systematic treatise; that many subjects occupy a space disproportionately large in its pages, and many others of greater moment are scarcely mentioned there; that the course of his argument, if that can strictly be called a course which is wholly destitute of method, is frequently embarrassed with long digressions, not always of much general value; that from his neglect of defining words used by him in new senses, the most diligent examiner is often at a loss to discover his meaning; finally, that in some fundamental matters, such as the operation of labor in giving value, the nature of wealth, its production, distribution, and consumption, his positions are unsound, by whatever theory they are tested.—A belief is entertained that the considerations adduced in the following pages will add to the catalogue of his admitted errors.

As Americans, also, we are all bound to take exception to his illiberal reflections on the dispute, which led to the revolutionary war, and on our causes of complaint against the mother country.—We have not been sufficiently awake to the mischievous effects of introducing many English writings into our seminaries of education, and of giving credence to their authors on subjects of political economy and politics.—It is a truism to say that our institutions are radically different from the English. Ours are throughout republican, theirs are substantially monarchical. Theirs are the oft-changed remnants of feudal barbarism ; ours are a great political invention, which undergoes its first trial in this country.—And yet we have Blackstone and Paley for our text books in politics, who, whatever may be their excellencies on other accounts, are certainly the bigoted advocates, the courtly apologists, of whatever, in the system of the British government, is corrupt in itself, and most adverse to the genius and principles of our own government.

And so also we take Smith as our *magnus Apollo* in political economy, the basis of whose theory is, that *the country-gentlemen*, that is, the landed aristocracy, of Britain, are the only class for whose benefit government is instituted, laws enacted, or who deserve the regard of the statesman, and that all the other productive classes, the mechanical, the manufacturing, the mercantile, are a set of sharpers, who have been constantly engaged, ever since the Conquest, in a conspiracy to defraud the simple, innocent, and defenceless country gentlemen, and to impoverish and ruin the country. These are strong terms, but they are not stronger than the text warrants. Now, although we have no order, which exactly corresponds to Smith's British *country-gentlemen*, yet, in the present relation, the partial and exclusive nature of such a theory as this would be less objectionable, were it not for his equally partial and exclusive views of the origin of the American war. We may be content to learn even from a foe ; but when we go to him for instruction, let us previously have a fair understanding upon the point. Surely it is not for our interest to allow the opinions of our national enemy to acquire a kind of prescriptive authority in the country.—It is not for our interest to place the writings of our national enemy in the hands of our youth, and thus administer, ourselves, poisoned aliment to the lips of the rising generation.

Many persons are accustomed to attribute a sort of oracular authority to Adam Smith, who never attentively perused the

Inquiry.—It may not be generally known, therefore, that he takes pains to ridicule our colonial legislatures as little knots of factious rebels; that he sneers at the high minded men, who composed our continental congress, as being upstart 'shop-keepers and attornies,' animated only with the little pride of becoming provincial dukes and marquises; and that he stigmatises, with the grossest terms of opprobrium, the master spirits of seventy-six, Washington and Adams, Franklin and Jefferson and their compeers, whose glorious names are and will be the watchword of millions, who shall never dream of the learned Glasgow sage's existence. Americans may not be apprised of these things; but they ought to be, ere they determine to repose implicit reliance upon the opinions of Adam Smith.

It would ill become an American of this day to argue with an Englishman of that, as to which country was right in the controversy of our independence.—Our cause has been stamped with the seal of justice by time and by heaven.—The vindication of the statesmen and heroes of sixty-five and seventy-four may, in this case, be safely left to history and to the hearts of our countrymen. The opinions of Adam Smith on this subject, are introduced here, not for the purpose of refuting them, for they do not deserve so much attention; but only to hold them up to the reprobation and indignation of an insulted people.

Let it be holden in remembrance then, that, in treating of colonies, he traduces, in good set phrases, the whole American people.

Let it be remembered, further, that he invidiously represents the metropolis as having sustained wars and heavy expenses for our defence.—Kind mother country! Ungrateful child!—The colonists come hither as exiles driven by oppression from their native land, the government of which, so far from assisting them to establish settlements here, would scarcely grant half the colonies even the poor boon of a charter.

Most of the New England colonies founded their governments without any legal authority so to do.—They fought their own way into consequence, unaided by the metropolis, although but a handful themselves, in the midst of warlike savages.—England took little notice of us until she found out we were thriving and industrious, and rapidly increasing in numbers. Then she graciously condescended to remodel our government, to appoint officers over us, and to receive the monopoly of our trade, authorising us to buy of her, and at her price, any commodity which we had means to buy withal, and to sell our own produce to her at such prices as she chose to give, provided we took especial care to produce nothing which she produced, or which could interfere with her manufactures, and provided we did not attempt to sell to any body else.—It so happened, likewise, that the French had made a little settlement in Canada and Acadia about the same time with the settlement of the English in New England and Virginia.—We did not interfere with each other. There was space enough in this vast continent for us both, and we were disposed to live amicably together. Indeed, a military expedition to Europe was quite as easy for us to make as one at that time from Boston to Quebec.—Now ever since the year 1066, when Britain was conquered by the Norman French, England was incessantly engaged in wars of invasion and aggression against France; and whenever they were at variance in Europe, they insisted that we should be likewise in America. We strained every nerve to comply with the requisitions of our mother-country, and were thus forced into idle contests, as causeless as they were calamitous, which well nigh made our governments bankrupt, inundated the country with a spurious and ruinous paper currency, and cut off our bravest men in battle.—And strange it was, according to Adam Smith, that, after receiving all these and a multitude other like blessings from England, we should refuse to submit to have her tax us, against our consent, for the supply of the wasteful and extravagant expenditure of her government, in carrying on wars to maintain the balance of Europe!

Let it be remembered, finally, that he attributes the war of independence to the intrigues of a few ambitious factionaries, and not to its true cause, the spontaneous throes of a nation resolved to be free.—Now, although we may pardon all this, considering that the cause of our country was misunderstood, and misrepresented in England when Adam Smith wrote, and that he would have written otherwise had he flourished fifty years later, yet it must be urged as detracting from his influence and merit in the eye of unprejudiced Americans.

Let us now proceed to examine some of the economical doctrines taught in the pages of the Inquiry

2. 'The real wealth of a country' consists in 'the exchangeable value of the annual produce of its land and labor.' These words, frequently employed by Dr. Smith, indicate the sense in which he appears generally to understand wealth, although he gives no precise definition of it. (*B.* II, *ch.* 3; and *B.* IV, *ch.* 3.)

He makes no distinction between wealth and value:—he does not seem to be aware that the wealth of a country might be diminished, while the sum total of its exchangeable values remained undiminished. (*Principles.*)

3. With respect to the increase of wealth, Dr. Smith considers what is saved from annual income and added to capital as the only source of it. (*B.* II, *ch.* 3.) He entirely overlooks the increasing value of all real property, which arises from the progress of industry and the increase of population, and which takes place in every country where industry is encouraged and protected.

In this country there are individuals, who, from the operation of these causes in raising the value of their lands, have, without saving from income to add to capital, arisen from small property to great wealth.

4. Dr. Smith, in treating of value, says it is of two kinds, 'value in use' and 'value in exchange,' (*B.* I, *ch.* 4): a distinction, which only serves to produce confused notions upon the nature of value.

In the use of a thing there is utility, but not value. Value arises only in exchange, and it is only by exchange that the value of things can be estimated. (*Principles.*)

5. Labor, he says, is 'the real measure of exchangeable value.' (*B.* I, *ch.* 5.) If so, why then do we not measure value by it? We do not value a thing by the labor, which it may have cost to produce it; nor by the labor which it will command. A commodity may have cost one man twice the labor to produce it, which it would have cost another*; and it may have cost in one place ten times the labor which it would have cost in another. On the other hand, a commodity may not command half as much labor as has been expended upon it, or it may command ten times as much, according to the circumstances of the case.

We value a commodity by the want or desire which we have for it, and not by the labor which it cost or will command. It is not labor, but the products of labor, which we want; and whether these products have cost more or less labor, or will command more or less, is a thing we do not inquire about. The only thing which concerns us, is the quantity of other products, which we must give in exchange to obtain those we want. And the only measure there is of the value of a particular commodity, is in the quantity of other commodities, which we must give for the purchase of it.

6. Adam Smith, when he says first, that 'labor is the real measure of the exchangeable value of commodities,' (*B.* I, *ch.* 5); and then again, that 'the real value of every commodity is finally measured and determined by the proportion which its average money-price bears to the average money-price of corn,' (*B.* I, *ch.* 5,) not only lays down erroneous principles, but principles inconsistent with each other.

How can labor and corn, when their fluctuations in value rarely if ever correspond one with the other, be both at the same time measures of the real value of commodities?

Or how can the proportion between the price of corn and the price of other commodities, which only determines the difference between the price of one commodity and the price of another, be the final measure of the real value of every commodity?

We measure the relative value of commodities by comparing the actual price of one with that of another; and we measure the actual price of a commodity by the quantity of money for which it may be exchanged.

But we cannot measure the actual or real value of a commodity, unless we could measure the actual value of the quantity of every other commodity which it could be purchased with; and this, unless the different kinds of commodities were limited to very few, would be impossible.

7. He further says, 'that the real price of a commodity is the labor it will command, and that the money it will command, is its nominal price only.' (*B.* I, *ch.* 5.) To the contrary of this, the real price of a commodity is the money it will command, and it has no other price.

The market-price of a commodity, he says, depends on demand, but 'the natural price depends on wages, profit, and rent.' (*B.* I, *ch.* 7.) The market-price of a commodity is the only natural price there is; and this naturally arises from our wants; and it is our wants alone, which can give to a commodity its price or value.

8. He makes a very useless division of the value of commodities into three parts, labor, rent, and profits; and says labor measures the value. (*B.* I, *ch.* 6.) Were this the case, and were it possible to ascertain in what proportion these parts entered to make up the value of a commodity, it could serve no practical purpose whatever. It could have no possible influence, either on demand or price.

9. He considers 'the acquired and useful abilities of all the inhabitants of the country,' as a portion of its 'fixed capital.' (*B.* II, *ch.* 1.) This is confounding things together, which are essentially and totally unlike in nature. He might as well consider the capacity to labor to be labor itself, or the ability to produce a commodity to be the commodity itself. The acquisition of skill, if employed in aid of labor, accelerates production; and the capital consists in the articles produced, and not in the skill aiding in their production.

Useful abilities, though not productively employed, may nevertheless be employed as beneficially for society, in proportion to the share they receive of the general product for their compensation, as are the abilities of those, who by their productive employments furnish this compensation; but neither the abilities of one nor of the other form any portion of the material and transferable property, in which fixed capital consists.

The skill and labor employed by one division of society produce wealth; the exercise of useful abilities by the other merely causes a portion of it to change owners, and pass from the possession of one to the possession of the other.

10. Smith does not seem to entertain very correct notions of what the general interest of society consists in, when he says that the interest of those who live by the profits of productive industry, namely, the tenant, the mechanic, the manufacturer, the merchant,—in short all, who use their intelligence, skill, and capital in the employment and support of labor, 'have not the same connexion with the general interest of society,' as the interests of those have, who live by *rent* and wages. How they, who live by rent, should contribute more to the public interest than they, who live by the profits of productive industry, is a thing which he does not condescend to explain. (*B.* I, *ch.* 10.)

11. Not only, however, does he represent the interest of those, who live by the profits of productive industry, as not the same

with that of the public, but also the interest of the towns, as different from, and even opposite to, that of the country. (*B.* I, *ch.* 10.)

The inhabitants of the towns, consisting principally of merchants, manufacturers, and mechanics, he represents as combining to secure to themselves the monopoly of the home-market, for the products of their different kinds of industry, against their own countrymen and foreigners both, by which they are enabled, he says, to sell those products dearer, to the injury of the country. (*B.* I, *ch.* 10, *pt.* 2.)

He accuses the mechanics of this combination because of their guild-regulations, which secure the acquisition of art, dexterity, and habits of industry, by long apprenticeships. He says that these lessen competition, and that, 'in the common mechanic trades, apprenticeships of a few days might certainly be sufficient!' (*B.* I, *ch.* 10, *pt.* 2.) Adam Smith could never have hazarded such a remark, if theory had not closed his ears to the lessons of experience. Is the habit of attentive, steady labor of no account? Is manual expertness nothing? Is a thorough knowledge of business and the details of a mechanic art useless? And yet the attainment of all these qualities is the work of time. There is no royal road to skill, practice, and habit.

He contrasts the inhabitants of the towns with the inhabitants of the country; but in saying that the 'country-gentlemen and farmers are least subject to this wretched spirit of monopoly,' (*B.* IV, *ch.* 2),—how could he gloss over the fact, that in England they first set the example of 'this wretched spirit,' by securing to themselves the entire monopoly of the home-market for their produce and that they still retained full possession of it, to the utter exclusion of meat and corn, not luxuries, but necessaries of life, produced in other countries?

12. The merchants and manufacturers, he condemns as being 'the original inventors of those restraints upon the importation of foreign goods, which secure to them the monopoly of the home market,' (*B.* IV, *ch.* 2):—a thing which seems to excite his utmost indignation.

The restraint upon the importation of foreign goods has its sole object to lead to the acquisition of that degree of skill which, as Smith himself admits, the same kind of goods r be made after a certain time as cheap at home as in the eign country. (B. IV, *ch.* 2.)

The manufacturer, by the skill acquired through the ation of these restraints, enables the merchant not only t ply the home-market with goods of home-manufacture ch than it could be supplied with like goods from abroad, bu to supply foreign markets with them cheaper than the before supplied with foreign goods.

The superior skill and diligence of the towns ren employment of both labor and capital in them more p than they are in the country. This he erroneously c to be an advantage gained by the towns to the injury country; and most zealously contends against the u only means, by which their skill and diligence are

13. 'Stock and labor,' he says, 'seek the mos tageous employment. They naturally therefore re town and desert the country.' (*B.* I, *ch.* 10, *pt.* 2.

In supposing the towns to attract capital from th and thereby injure the interests of the country, double error. In the first place, the towns can capital from the country; in the second, if they would not injure the interests of the country by do

The capital in agriculture is chiefly fixed. It live-stock, and implements of husbandry. This not 'desert the country and resort to the town more advantageous employment there.'

As for that portion of the agricultural capital, w in the produce of the land,—the more of it there sorts to the towns and deserts the country,' th it takes from the towns to be employed and country.

And with respect to the laborers, both the

That every increase or d diminishes the number of pr

That this capital, whatever it employs, are all divided be and commerce :—

The capital in agriculture i to the labor it employs, than or commerce. (*B.* II, *ch.* 5) :—

That high duties, prohibitio to protect against foreign com home-trade, are, as he calls t manufacture and commerce :—

That they turn capital from able employment of it, to man productive employments of it :—

That they diminish thereby t and are consequently hurtful regu

His notion that no country poss ploy all its labor is obviously u means of employing labor are o subsistence; and every country ploying every individual, which it

Every country must support al employs them or not; and to emp tal beyond their support; for the t materials to work upon, the very plies.

It is not from the want of means the want of motives to labor, that The labor itself, while employed, wi capital necessary for its own maint yond, for accumulation.

Smith is equally unsupported by capital in agriculture is more product employments. That it is not so is to monstration. It is sufficient to observe that the income from agricultural capital, that is to say, the rent of land and the profits of its employment, is less than the interest of money and the profits of the employment of circulating capital, in every country.

Capital cannot be turned from agriculture to commerce and manufacture. Land cannot be put in circulation; and to leave it uncultivated would be to sink the capital. Therefore the regulations, which he decries, cannot have the effect which he attributes to them.

The effect, which these regulations in reality have, is this, —that by increasing the quantity of product in the branches of industry which they encourage, they augment thereby the value of products in every other branch, and thus make considerable addition to the exchangeable value of the annual product of labor and capital.

16. The following extracts show the difference between the results of Adam Smith's reasoning, and the results of his observation. Reasoning from false premises leads him to false conclusions; observation presents him facts.

In one place he asserts that 'The capital employed in agriculture not only puts in motion a greater quantity of productive labor than any equal capital employed in manufactures, but in proportion, too, to the quantity of productive labor which it employs, it adds a much greater value to the annual produce of the land and labor of the country, to the real wealth and revenue of its inhabitants. Of all ways in which capital can be employed, it is by far the most advantageous to the society.' (*B.* II, *ch.* 5.) And in another he observes that 'The profits of agriculture seem to have no superiority over those of other employments in any part of Europe.' (*B.* II, *ch.* 5.)

Again he says that, 'Upon equal or nearly equal profits most men will choose to employ their capitals rather in the improvement and cultivation of land than either in manufactures or foreign trade,' (*B.* III, *ch.* 1); and further that 'Agriculture is almost every where capable of absorbing a much greater capital than has ever yet been employed in it.' (*B.* II, *ch.* 5.) Now if capital in agriculture affords such a superior profit as he says it does, and men prefer this employment of capital with equal profit, it is a thing altogether inconceivable that agriculture should every where want capital.

17. Smith seems to ascribe to capital the functions, which belong only to labor. That it is capital which begets labor, instead of labor capital,—that capital is the cause rather than the effect of labor,—that more labor cannot be employed in agriculture without more capital,—these are the radical errors, which pervade all his reasonings upon the employment of labor, and which lead him to his erroneous conclusions.

The preceding year's produce supplies all the capital necessary for the support of the present year's labor; and if more labor is not employed in agriculture, it is not because there is a want of means, but because there is a want of inducement to employ it, namely, the inducement, which consists in the profits of its employment.

18. Although Smith declaims with so much earnestness against those 'human institutions, which disturb the natural course of things,' yet he does not seem to be very consistent in his opinions concerning their effect. For in speaking of towns he says that, 'If human institutions had never thwarted the natural inclinations of man, the towns could no where have increased beyond what the improvement and cultivation of the territory in which they were situated could support,' (*B.* III, *ch.* 1): yet again he says, 'Through the greater part of Europe the commerce and manufactures of cities, instead of being the effect, have been the cause and occasion of the improvement and cultivation of the country.' (*B.* III, *ch.* 4.)

Nor does he seem to have any very great objection to the application of the principles of those regulations, 'which disturb the natural order of things,' to agriculture. He first observes that 'The law of England favors agriculture not only indirectly by the protection of commerce, but by several direct encouragements. Those who cultivate the land have a monopoly against their countrymen for the two greatest and most important articles of land produce, bread and butcher's meat.' (*B.* III, *ch.* 4.) And he then asks, 'What would agriculture have been, had the law given no direct encouragement to it, besides what arises indirectly from the progress of commerce, and had left the yeomanry in the same condition as in most other countries in Europe?' (*B.* III, *ch.* 4.)

But without much regard to consistency of opinion in respect of these regulations in their general application, he asserts that, 'By restraining, either by high duties or by absolute prohibitions, the importation of such goods from foreign countries as can be produced at home, the monopoly of the home market is more or less secured to the domestic industry employed in producing them,—a monopoly against their own countrymen.' (*B.* IV, *ch.* 2.) This is not a correct statement of the thing. It is, on the contrary, a monopoly in favor of all the inhabitants of the country which grants it, against the inhabitants of all foreign countries. The branches of industry, to which the home-market is secured, are open to every individual of the country. These branches, therefore, can possess no monopoly against the individuals employed in other branches.

19. He further contends that, 'The general industry of the society never can exceed what the capital of the society can employ;'—that 'No regulation can increase the quantity of industry in any society beyond what its capital can maintain;' and that such regulations 'can only divert a part of it into a direction into which it might not otherwise have gone.' (*B.* IV, *ch.* 2.) To this it may be answered that all the inhabi-

tants of a country are maintained by its capital, whether employed or not; that it requires no more capital to support them in idleness than to employ them in industry; and that if regulations to encourage industry divert a portion of capital in a direction into which it would not otherwise have gone, it is from one employment to another employment which is more profitable; and that the employment which it has left is rendered more profitable by its departure, as the competition in it is thereby lessened.

20. He asserts, that 'Every individual is continually exerting himself to find out the most advantageous employment for whatever capital he can command;' and that 'The study of his own advantage naturally, or rather necessarily, leads him to prefer that employment, which is most advantageous to the society.' (*B.* IV, *ch.* 2.).

If this be true, an individual, who employs his capital in speculating or gambling, employs it in a manner the most advantageous to society. But it is not true; and Smith lies under mistake in supposing it would be advantageous to the community that every individual should be left to employ his capital where he might find it most profitable to himself, unless every individual of the community were equally independent of each other individual, and no one dependant on others for employment and support. For unless such were the case, if those who possessed the capital were to use it for the employment of foreign labor, because it was cheaper, the laborers of the country, being left without employment, must come upon the community for support.

21. Again, Smith asserts that, 'To give the monopoly of the home-market to the produce of domestic industry in any particular art or manufacture, is in some measure to direct private people in what manner they ought to employ their capitals, and must in almost all cases be either a useless or a hurtful regulation.' (*B.* IV. *ch.* 2.) This regulation does not in any measure direct private people in what manner they

ought to employ their capitals. It leaves to every individual the same employment unimpaired for his capital, which he had before, and with full liberty to turn a part of it, if he please, to the new employment, which if he should do, the whole capital would be more profitably employed than it was before. Furthermore, the regulation is neither a hurtful nor a useless one. It is on the contrary a beneficial one. It increases industry, not only in the branch which is the object of encouragement, but it likewise occasions an increase of products in every other branch. The increase of products in any one branch of industry increases the quantities of commodities to be given in exchange for the products of the other branches.

22. Smith admits, however, that 'By such regulations a particular manufacture may sometimes be acquired sooner than it would have been otherwise, and after a certain time may be made at home as cheap or cheaper than in the foreign country.' (*B.* IV, *ch.* 2.) But then he assumes what follows: 'The industry of the society can augment only in proportion as its capital augments, and its capital can augment only in proportion to what can be gradually saved out of its revenue. But the immediate effect of every such regulation is to diminish its revenue, and what diminishes its revenue is certainly not very likely to augment its capital faster than it would have augmented of its own accord, had both capital and industry been left to find out their natural employments.' (*B.* IV, *ch.* 2.)

And why is it, as he admits, that after a certain time goods may be manufactured at home as cheap as in the foreign country? Why, because at home, after a certain time, encouraged by such regulations as he condemns, an equal or superior degree of perfection may be attained in the machinery, and an equal or superior degree of skill and dexterity attained in its management in manufacture, compared with what has been attained in these respects in the foreign country.

23. He asserts that the immediate effect of every such

regulation is to diminish the income of society; and that it diminishes it, because, as he assumes, its capital can employ only a certain quantity of labor; and thence he concludes, that 'Had capital and the labor it employs been left to find out their natural employments, the capital would have augmented faster of his own accord.' (*B.* IV, *ch.* 2.) Thus, according to this doctrine, ordinary manual labor, left to seek its own employment, is more productive of wealth to the nation than skilled labor is, when aided by the powers of nature and machinery in production.

24. He further asserts that, 'Though for want of such regulations the society should never acquire the proposed manufacture, it would not upon that account necessarily be the poorer in any one period of its duration.' And he endeavors to prove the assertion by the following very logical arguments: 'In every period of its duration, its whole capital and industry might still have been employed, though upon different objects, in the manner that was most advantageous at the time. In every period its revenue might have been the greatest, which its capital could afford, and both capital and revenue might have been augmented with the greatest possible rapidity.' (*B.* IV, *ch.* 2.)

If mere manual labor can at any period of the duration of society be employed to as much advantage as skilled labor aided by the powers of nature and machinery can, then may capital and income be augmented by mere manual labor, at every period, with as great rapidity as they are augmented by the combined powers of nature, art, and labor directed by skill; but not otherwise.

25. Adam Smith argues that, 'If a foreign country can supply us with a commodity cheaper than we ourselves can make it, better buy it of them with some part of the produce of our own industry employed in a way in which we have some advantage.' (*B.* IV, *ch.* 2.) But what if the foreign country would not take this produce in payment for their com-

modity? Yet if they would, it would not be better to buy it of them, than to make it ourselves, unless the whole labor of the country were fully employed, and not only fully employed but employed in the most advantageous manner. This, however, is not the case in any country. At least it is not our case. Therefore, as a portion of our people are unemployed, or only partly employed, it would be better for the nation to employ them in making the commodity, which otherwise would be bought of a foreign country. For it is clear that, by so doing, the value of it, let the commodity cost whatever time it might in making, would be so much saved to the nation.

It never can be for the interest of a nation to import commodities from foreign countries merely because they are produced there by superior skill, and therefore cheaper, than if produced by its own labor. Rather than do this, a nation ought, in regard to its interest, to adopt such measures as would, through the encouragement they afforded, lead to the acquisition of the skill, by which, when acquired, the commodities would be made within itself to cost less than if imported from the foreign country.

26. In respect of commerce Smith observes that, 'Whether the capital which carries the surplus produce of a country abroad be a foreign or a domestic one, is of very little importance.' (*B.* II, *ch.* 5.) He is mistaken. It is of so much importance as this, that in one case the amount of freight and the commercial profit would be lost to the country, and in the other case it would be gained. The labor of no country is so fully employed as not to be capable of supplying the means of carrying its surplus produce to market.

27. Smith further observes in respect of commerce, that 'The trade to the East Indies, by opening a market for the commodities of Europe, or *what comes nearly to the same thing*, to the gold and silver which is purchased with those commodities, must necessarily tend to increase the annual production of European commodities, and consequently the real wealth and revenue of Europe.' (*B.* IV, *ch.* 1.)

It is not 'nearly the same thing' to Europe to employ gold and silver in this trade as to employ her own commodities. There is the greatest difference in the result. America, from which the gold and silver are purchased, will not consume more European commodities in consequence of Europe's consuming more India-commodities, and Europe herself must necessarily consume less. The India-silk and cotton goods, which she consumes, must prevent the consumption of an equal quantity of European silk and cotton goods. And unless the consumption of European-commodities be increased by the European consumption of India-commodities, it is impossible that the exportation of gold or silver from Europe to India for their purchase, can increase the production of European commodities.

But if, instead of sending the gold or silver to India, this were employed in the purchase of European products, and these products were sent to India for the purchase of India-goods, the exportation of these European products would then cause the additional production of an equal quantity to replace them in the European market.

Thus it appears that when gold or silver is exported in this trade, no additional consumption of home-products is the consequence of it, and therefore that no increased home-production could possibly arise from it. Whereas when home-products are exported, an additional consumption is the consequence of it, and an increased production follows to replace in the home-market the quantity taken out for exportation.

In both cases, the same quantity of India-goods returns, and there is at the same time an equal quantity of home-products in the market; but in the first case the gold or silver remains in India; in the latter case it remains at home.

The difference then between the two cases is this: that the money in one case is expended, and in the other case it is saved; and the exporting nation is, to the amount of the money saved, so much richer in one case than it would have been in the other.

To purchase with money and consume the products of a foreign nation, which does not receive and consume our products, causes no additional consumption of our products, and consequently cannot lead to any additional production. But to import and consume the products of a foreign nation, which receives and consumes our products in exchange for them, does cause an additional consumption of our products, and consequently leads to an additional production for its supply.

28. Smith says: 'It is the maxim of every prudent master of a family never to attempt to make at home what it will cost him more to make than to buy.—What is prudence in the conduct of every private family can scarce be folly in that of a great kingdom.' (*B.* IV, *ch.* 2.)

This analogy does not always hold good, or rather the policy of a family is sometimes different from what it is conceived to be by Smith.

The fallacy of the argument is this. The opponents to the system of protecting domestic industry treat the subject, in this case, not in its relation to the interest of a single nation, but in its relation to the general interests of industry all over the world. But their own illustration is against their theory.

The master of a family, say they, will not attempt to make his own clothes, shoes, hat, furniture, house, and so forth. The progress of society has introduced the division of labor, and it is clearly for his advantage to confine his own labor to arts in which he is an adept, and wherein he has full employment, by means whereof he can produce a greater quantity of exchangeable values, in the aggregate, than if his attention and skill were parcelled out among various callings. Therefore the tailor buys his shoes of the shoemaker, and the shoemaker employs the tailor to make his coat.

The world consists of a multitude of industrious nations, separated by their respective peculiar institutions, but united again by the common benefits of mutual commerce, and each eager to surpass the other in the acquisition of wealth. Each nation is composed of many states, provinces, or other large communities. Each of these, is subdivided into numerous cities, towns, or villages; each city into circles of associated friends, or of families, connected together by ties of relationship or otherwise; and lastly these circles into separate families or households.

Now, to begin with an association of friends or families, if we suppose them to be governed by a single head, or to act by conference and in concert, and to aim to promote *primarily* the interest of their own circle, what should be their policy? If their number contained various branches of industrious arts, would not their interests as a body dictate to them to purchase of each other, and to employ the productive industry of each other, rather than to purchase of another body of men, and employ their productive industry? Or if their number contained many idle hands, or hands imperfectly employed, would not the interest of the association demand that their idle hands, or hands imperfectly employed, should be encouraged in setting up some profitable trade, by having the association restricted to make its purchases within itself, rather than of other traders?

Or take the stronger case of a city, which is composed of a great variety of traders and artists of every description, and also contains idle and waste hands, and perhaps many paupers. How shall such a city best promote its single municipal interest, supposing that politically it has power to adopt or impose the necessary policy? It will, in the first place, require that all the inhabitants shall purchase the products of the industry of the city exclusively, provided the requisite commodities are produced within it. Next, if the inhabitants of the place have been accustomed to purchase certain products elsewhere, and some one inhabitant is ready to undertake to employ the spare labor of the community in the domestic production of such commodities, all the other inhabitants of the city will be required to purchase of him alone; certain that, if the price is, for a short time, higher than the price of the foreign commodity, this price will soon be reduced by the competition of the other inhabitants, who will undertake to produce the same commodity. We may rest assured that idleness would soon be converted to industry, poverty would disappear, and general prosperity prevail, in the city which should have courage to adopt, and vigor to maintain such regulations.

But this, it will be said, is a monopoly. True, it is a monopoly of domestic industry against foreign, a monopoly in favor of all the inhabitants of the city, against the inhabitants of all other cities. But it is not a monopoly in favor of any individual inhabitant of the city. Perfect freedom of trade and industry exist within it, only protected from external competition.

It is clear that, in each of these cases, the policy supposed is beneficial to the family or association of individuals, who seek to advance their own interest by mutual protection, and to the city, which seeks the same protection for its own inhabitants. And it is equally so for the nation, which desires to protect the interest of its own people against the competition of foreign nations.

OBSERVATIONS

ON

SAY'S POLITICAL ECONOMY.

---

1. The treatise on Political Economy, by Jean Baptiste Say, has been received very favorably both in Europe and America. The principles of Say are essentially those of Adam Smith. The source of his popularity was evidently the want, which the public had long so sensibly felt, of any suitable treatise on the science of political economy. Say, however, very modestly claims for his work the distinction of supplying this *desideratum* perfectly ; with how much reason, the reader will be more competent to judge correctly after perusing the following pages.

The ensuing criticisms upon this work may appear to some persons, who have inconsiderately taken up the common idea with regard to its author, as somewhat close and severe. Nor would the scrutiny have been conducted so narrowly, but for the peculiar circumstances of the case. His work has been published in this country in an English translation, and is pretty frequently holden up to the community as a text-book of sound elementary principles. The matter has been carried so far that several of our literary institutions have adopted it, as a class book in political economy. When a book so confused in its arrangement, so mistaken in fundamental doctrines, and teaching opinions prejudicial to the welfare of this country, is made a part of the course of study in our colleges, there would seem to be urgent occasion for a strict examination of its qualities and tendency to be made.

The governors of those institutions deserve much commendation for causing instruction to be given in a science so important to be generally understood, and hitherto so little studied, as the nature and causes of national wealth. The months, nay the years, generally spent by all without distinction, in poring over pages of Greek, Latin, or mathematics, which few of the students comprehend, and fewer still have any occasion in after life to apply, might better be appropriated to the acquisition of the modern languages and of sciences of immediate, universal, constant, practical utility. It may be long, indeed, before our colleges will completely escape from the operation of those influences, which now divert them so widely from the proper objects of lay-education. While, therefore, every indication, which they give of conformity to the spirit of the times, ought to be encouraged by the public applause, and while the improvement in question is especially laudable, it is to be regretted that a treatise so exceptionable in its principles and arrangement as Say's should be put in the hands of students, whom it would be better to leave uninstructed than to fill their minds with pernicious errors.

The design of the subsequent remarks, so far as they may exercise any influence, is to counteract the injurious effects, which the popularity of this book would be likely to exert upon the interests of America. Passing over many incorrect observations and theoretical notions in it, which have connexion rather with the vanity of authorship than with the professed object of the author's work, the tenor of these remarks will be principally confined to what is erroneous in principle and theory, to such doctrines as are opposed to means by which public prosperity is promoted, and to such principles as would in their practical application be detrimental to the welfare of the nation. Two or three remarks are also subjoined upon Mr. Biddle's notes to the American edition of Say's work.

2. The extraordinary presumption manifested by Say in his introduction, affords no very favorable presage of the subsequent tenor of the book. After pointing out the absurdities, errors, fallacies, and deficiences of all previous systems of political economy, he kindly gives the reader to understand that, as 'We are not yet in possession of an established text-book on the science of political economy, in which the fruits of an enlarged and accurate observation are referred to general principles, that might be admitted by every reflecting mind,'— he will favor us with such a work, one 'so complete and well arranged,' that it 'might every where and at all times be studied with advantage.' And then with great self-complacency he adds that, 'to prepare himself for undertaking so useful a task, he thought it necessary to examine attentively what had been previously written on the same subject, and afterwards to forget it!' (*Int. p.* lvii.)

Being thus prepared, he goes on to say that 'it was but reasonable to expect from the lights of the age, and from the method of philosophizing, which has so powerfully contributed to the advancement of other sciences, that he might at all times be able to ascend to the nature of things, and never lay down an abstract principle that was not immediately applicable to practice.' Most logical and 'reasonable' conclusions these! That because the age was enlightened, we must admit his ability to ascend to the nature of things; and that by forgetting what others taught, he should therefore never lay down an abstract principle, which was not immediately applicable to practice. (*Int. p.* lvii.)

With such facility it is that Say comes to his general conclusions, not only, as in this case, with regard to the excellency of his book, but also in respect of the principles unfolded and discussed in it.

3. Nor is he less happy in the promptness, with which he

adjusts his general propositions to his intended conclusions. As for example, when, after having concluded that the rise of some modern states to opulence and power was not owing to the regulations for the encouragement of domestic industry which he opposes, but in spite of them, he advances the following inapplicable, inconsistent, and absurd propositions in support of his conclusion.

The first is, that 'Nations seldom derive any benefit from the lessons of experience.' This is inapplicable, first, because the experience of all nations is against his conclusion, and next because some nations prove by their opulence and power that they do know how to profit by the lessons of experience.

His second proposition is, that 'To profit by them the community at large must be enabled to seize the connexion between causes and their consequences, which at once supposes a very high degree of intelligence and a rare capacity for reflection.' This is not only inconsistent with fact, since men of all degrees of intellect, and even some brutes, can profit by experience, but also inconsistent with his next proposition, which is remarkable for its absurdity.

It is, that 'Whenever mankind shall be in a situation to profit by experience, they will no longer require her lessons; plain, sound sense will then be sufficient.' Without disputing that Say might conceit himself beyond profiting by experience, yet the world at large, or 'the unthinking multitude,' will be so perverse as to exercise their common sense, and treat with scorn the opinion that they are incapable of profiting by experience. And notwithstanding his high authority to the contrary, they will believe that 'plain, sound sense,' is wanting and cannot exist, where the man is beyond profiting 'by the lessons of experience.' (*Int. p.* xxx, *note.*)

4. Say proposes, as the object of his work, to unfold the manner in which wealth is produced, distributed, and consumed.

He proceeds to the execution of this purpose by dividing the work into three books, in the first of which he professes to treat of the production of wealth, in the second of its distribution, and in the third of its consumption. But the division he thus makes of his subject is merely nominal; for we find him under the necessity of treating of production, distribution, and consumption, in each of the three books, as being things inseparably connected with and dependant on each other, in their relation to national wealth.

Production, distribution, and consumption, though to be treated of together, should nevertheless be treated of as distinct things. Say, however, has, in the prosecution of his work confounded one with another in such a manner as greatly to perplex and confuse the reader.

In one place (I, 10) he designates an act of exchange as *production;* in another (II, 168) an act of purchase, which is the same thing as an act of exchange, he calls an act of *consumption.* Thus he makes what is in truth the distribution of commodities, to be at the same time both the production and the consumption of commodities.

He further tells us (II, 163) that 'a product consumed is a value lost to all the world and to all eternity.' Consequently, if, according to his doctrine, an act of purchase is an act of consumption, it must follow that a commodity is no sooner purchased than its value is annihilated to all eternity! He adds, however, after saying that an act of purchase is an act of consumption, that every act of resale is an act of reproduction. But the first proposition is made none the less absurd, by laying down another equally so to correspond with it. The commodity was not consumed by its purchase; nor was its value annihilated in the interval between its purchase and resale.

5. Products result from production; and in this connexion only should the term products be used, in speaking of the products of labor in their relation to the production of wealth.

Yet Say has what he terms immaterial products, a kind of product in which he admits capital cannot be accumulated, and consequently composing no part of what is called wealth. (I, 88, 89, 91.)

The remuneration of daily labor he calls a product, as well as that which is the object of labor. This is making labor doubly as productive as the 'unthinking' world has been accustomed to consider it. (*Ibid.*)

Further, he calls the fruits of prostitution a product, though, as he observes, of a very coarse and primitive kind of industry, by way of distinguishing it, as we are to suppose, from other products of industry, which he appears to consider of a finer and more recent kind. This latter sort of product, he has placed among his immaterial products, without being aware, perhaps, that he was giving it a pretty substantial form. (I, 94.)

6. In respect to capital, which consists in that portion of wealth which is employed by industry in production, Say treats of its nature and functions in a manner so loose and indefinite, as to render it impossible to acquire from his book any precise notions of what is to be understood by it.

He has his productive capital, and his unproductive capital, and other kinds of capital besides. The ability of the public functionary, he calls 'an accumulated capital;' (I, 93) and 'a full grown man,' he calls an accumulated capital also. (II,75.) Now as that which is essential to the character of capital, namely, its use in the employment of labor in production, is wanting in the three latter of these conditions, in which he supposes capital to exist, he not only mistakes the character of capital, but also that of the objects to which he applies it, in considering both one and the other to be the same thing.

7. In regard to wealth, Say in his definition of it does not seem to be aware of the distinction there is between that and value. He confounds wealth and value. 'Wealth,' he says, 'is proportionate to the quantum of value; great, when the aggregate of component value is great,—small, when the aggregate is small.' (I, 1.)

The distinction between wealth and value will appear in the following case. Suppose, for instance, that the harvest of a country were to fall short so far as to double the value of grain.

This would reduce the value of every other commodity in relation to grain one half. Here the relative values of commodities would be changed, but the sum-total of their values would not be diminished. The real wealth of the country, however, would be diminished. It would not employ the same quantity of labor, nor support the same number of persons; and unless the country should employ a part of its wealth to supply by importation the deficiency there may be for subsistence, a portion of its population would perish.

8. 'Price,' says Say, 'is the measure of the value of things, and their value the measure of utility.' (I, 3.) Here he errs in both propositions. Price is not the measure of the value of things. It only measures their value in relation to money. The value of things in their relation one to another is determined by the exchange of one thing for another. Neither is value the measure of utility; for the utility of a thing is measured only by its use.

9. 'Exchangeable value or price,' Say again observes, 'is an index of the recognised utility of a thing so long as human dealings are exempt from every influence but that of identical utility.' (I, 3.) Exchangeable value or price is *never* an index of the recognized utility of a thing. The value or price of wheat may be doubled by its scarcity, but its utility in use will not be doubled thereby. The exchangeable value of water is nothing; and yet what is there of greater utility?

10. He further says: 'There is no actual production of wealth without a creation or augmentation of utility.' (I, 4.) This is not correct. We know by experience that the exportation of wheat will produce in return twice as much wealth at one time as at another; but not in consequence of the 'augmentation of utility;' for the utility of wheat, in its use, is the same at all times.

11. Say, in making the observation, that 'without money to facilitate the interchange of products, production could never make any progress,' (I, 17,) seems to forget that products might be exchanged for each other, or that credit

might be substituted to a great extent for money to facilitate the interchange.

12. 'National industry,' Say asserts, 'is limited, not by territorial extent, but by extent of capital.' (I, 26.) This error he has adopted from Adam Smith. National industry is not limited by extent of capital. It is limited only by the want of inducements to employment.

The produce of the preceding year supplies the means of the present year's support, to all the inhabitants of the nation,—to those who are idle, as well as to those who labor; and there is no capital needed beyond this, for the full employment of the labor of the nation. The tools to work with, and the materials to work upon, labor produces for itself.

Therefore when the labor of a country is not fully employed, it is not from a deficiency of capital, or the want of the means of support; but it is because the profits of industry are not sufficient to afford to labor a renumeration ample enough to call it fully into action.

13. Say entertains a very singular notion upon the origin of husbandry. He observes that 'The first stage towards the attainment of wheat or wine was the discovery, by the natural philosopher or geologist, of the conduct and course of nature in the production of grain or the grape.' (I, 29.) Thus, in Say's opinion, before mankind had bread to eat or wine to drink, they must have had natural philosophers and geologists among them to teach them how to direct the course of nature in the production of the grain and the grape!

14. Say, in treating upon the division of labor, observes that the consequence of it is, to the individual, a degeneracy from the dignity of human nature, and a degradation of the faculties of the mind; and that, 'To have never done any thing but make the eighteenth part of a pin is a sorry account for a human being to give of his existence.'

(I, 65.) These are flippant observations, and made without the consideration that it was owing to this very division of labor that he was of a condition of life, which enabled him to talk of 'the dignity of human nature.'

Degeneracy cannot possibly proceed from useful industry. It is only by means of idleness, and the vices to which this leads, that mankind can become degenerate. Industry, by withholding them from vice, preserves them from degeneracy.

It is a necessary condition of the existence of man, that he should labor for its support; and in acting in conformity to this condition prescribed by nature, there is neither degeneracy nor degradation. Indeed, nature has made the physical well-being of man, and his intellectual improvement, depend upon his observance of it.

His labor, unaided by skill, with difficulty furnishes him the bare necessaries of life. It leaves him no leisure for the improvement of his mind. It is only through the division of labor that man acquires the skill, by which he directs his labors with the greater effect to the multiplication of its products; and it is only through this that he acquires the means, which afford him leisure for applying himself to the cultivation of his intellectual faculties. And it is inconsistent with the general provisions of nature that the progress of industry to that state, which alone admits of the cultivation of mind, should, as Say supposes, lead to degeneracy.

It is by man's confining his attention to the execution of single objects, whether of a material or intellectual nature, that his progress in arts, science, literature, and knowledge is so rapid. In proportion as the division of labor enables man to contribute more towards the general subsistence, and to the increase of knowledge, in the same proportion does it place more within the reach of every individual, not only the means of a comfortable living, but also the means of extending his general knowledge.

There is nothing, indeed, in general manual labor, which

has much tendency to enlarge the mind; but in the division of labor, where the single operations are performed habitually and unconsciously, the mind is left more at liberty to be employed in reflection or exercised in conversation. The more labor is limited to a particular object, the less attention will it require, and the more the mind will be left disengaged and free to be employed upon other objects. The fallacy of Say's reasoning upon this subject consists in his supposing the mind to be wholly employed, where only the hands are employed. A single operation, frequently repeated, is at length continued without a thought respecting it.

Whatever may be the general information of a person, who is regularly employed in any division of labor, it is probably greater than it would have been had he been unemployed. The degree of his information, however, depends more upon the manner of his bringing up, the character of his mind, and the kind of society he is in, than it does upon the particular mode of his employment.

15. Say again observes, in relation to capital, that 'The carrying trade is but little suited to nations possessed of small capital, whereof the whole is wanted to give activity to internal industry, which is always entitled to the preference.' (I, 64.) This observation results from his notion that industry is limited by capital, which is not correct. The activity of the internal industry of a country is in proportion to the profits it affords, and not to the quantity of capital which the country may possess. However small the capital of a country may be, it will always be sufficient for the employment of all its labor, whenever the employment of it affords an adequate and secure profit.

Indeed, the labor itself, while thus employed, produces not only all the capital necessary for the continuance of its own employment, but a surplus beyond, towards the accumulation of capital.

16. In respect to the effects of individual expenditure,

Say says, that 'The opulent individual, who vests 100,000 francs in gilding, plate, and the splendor of his establishment, has it not to lay out at interest, and withdraws it from the support of industry of any kind. The nation loses the annual revenue of so much capital, and the annual profit of the industry it might have kept in activity.' (I, 88.)

This is a great error, which runs through his whole work. He considers individual expenditure in all cases to be to the amount of it so much lost to the nation: whereas it is only an exchange of values, by which each party gets that which he values at more than he does what he gave for it. In this case the opulent individual has changed his 100,000 francs for other products of labor, which to him have an equal value; and though he no longer has the money to lay out at interest, yet those, who receive it from him for the products of their labor, have it, and are not likely to employ it less productively than he who parted with it would have done; and the nation loses nothing, either in capital or revenue, by the money having thus changed hands.

It is by the general expenditure, which is ever in proportion to the general income, that capital is kept in circulation, and industry in all its branches supported and encouraged.

17. Say advances propositions with respect to demand, which are at variance with uniform experience. He states, without limitation or exception, that 'It is production, which opens a demand for products;' that 'A product is no sooner created, than it from that instant opens a market for other products to the full extent of its own value;' that 'The mere circumstance of the creation of one product immediately opens a vent for other products;' and that 'The consumption of a product is the stoppage of a vent for them.' (I. 108, 111, 118.)

These are not true as general propositions. They are not true in respect to the perishable products of agriculture, where there is already in the market as great a quantity, as can be consumed within the time in which they can be kept from perishing. When this is the case, no additional production of them opens a vent for other products. Neither are they true with respect to any article, of which the production already exceeds the demand. They are true only in regard to such products as there may be a demand for.

18. He goes on to observe that, 'Having once arrived at the clear conviction that the general demand for produce is brisk in proportion to the activity of production, we need not trouble ourselves much to inquire towards what channel of industry production may be most advantageously directed.' (I, 118.) This is a conviction, at which the agriculturists of the United States will not very speedily arrive. Say's authoritative assertion will not convince them, contrary to their uniform experience, that the demand for their produce will be greater in proportion as they raise a greater quantity.

19. 'By the absolute exclusion of specific manufactures of foreign fabric,' says Say, 'a government establishes a monopoly in favor of the home-producers of those articles, and in prejudice of the home-consumers.' (I, 149.)

If a government excludes specific manufactures of foreign fabric, it is for the purpose of raising up the manufacture of similar fabrics at home, and for giving thereby to the inhabitants of the country the profit of supplying the home-market with them, instead of giving it to foreigners. In doing this, the government does not establish a monopoly in favor of a particular class in the country to the prejudice of other classes, by excluding foreign competition from the home-market. But it establishes a new branch of industry for the supply of the home-market, and a branch open for every individual of the country to enter into it, and avail himself of its advantages if he chooses.

If this deserve to be called a monopoly, it is a monopoly in favor of all the inhabitants of the country, which establishes it, against the inhabitants of all foreign countries.

A nation rarely, if ever, prohibits the introduction of foreign fabrics, except when it possesses natural advantages for producing them within itself equal to those of foreign countries, but is only deficient in a certain degree of skill, with which, if the nation possessed it, the fabrics would be produced at home for as cheap a price as that for which they could be introduced from abroad.

It is, then, with a just regard to its own interests, that a nation adopts those regulations, through which alone, by the protection and encouragement they afford, the requisite degree of skill is acquired.

In the acquisition of this, its industry is not only rendered more productive, but more active in all its various branches.

20. Say advances further, in relation to the same subject, that 'If the articles be not wholly prohibited, but merely saddled with an import duty, the home-producers can then increase their price by the whole amount of the duty,' and the consumer will have to pay the difference out of his pocket as a 'premiun to the home manufacturer.' (I, 150.)

This assertion is not true; and that it is not, we have the most complete proof in our own experience. Several years ago, our government increased the import duty on cotton goods of the more ordinary kinds to the amount of fifty per cent. and upwards.

This great increase of duty did not, even from the first, raise the price of these goods in any sensible degree. Yet, by the protection which it afforded to our capital against foreign competition, it led to a domestic competition in their manufacture, by which a degree of perfection has been attained in the machinery, and skill acquired in its management, which enable the home manufacturer to supply the consumer with them at a lower rate than he would have been supplied for, had not the duty been increased on their importation.

The fallacy of Say's reasoning against public regulations for the encouragement of domestic industry, consists in his not noticing their obvious effect to increase domestic production, not only in articles which are the object of restraint, but in all other articles in every branch of industry previously established;—and in his not noticing the effect they have, by the competition to which they give rise among the producers of the articles of which the importation has been restrained, to lower the price of the domestic article below what was previously paid for the imported one. (*B.* I, *ch.* 17.)

21. Say adopts the notions of Adam Smith as to the effect of regulations restraining and prohibiting the import of foreign manufactures, for the purpose of encouraging manufacture at home. But, in his reasoning to establish his positions on this subject, he has come to conclusions totally inconsistent with the 'wonderful increase of opulence,' which he previously represents as having resulted from the introduction of the cotton manufacture and calico-printing into France by means of regulations of this nature.

On this occasion he speaks with admiration of the 'firmness and extensive information,' which upheld the administration against the loud remonstrances of the *merchants*, and the general clamor in opposition to the establishment of these manufactures in France. (I, 130, 131.)

Nor does he seem very consistent, when, in terms of commendation, he represents the minister of France, by his protection of manufactures, 'as placing vast resources at the disposal of his sovereign,' (I, 13,) and multiplying, by that mean, these 'resources faster than the court squandered them;' (I, 82,) particularly considering that the protection, which the minister afforded, consisted in prohibitions of foreign manufactures, and bounties on the home manufacture.

Nor is he any more consistent with himself in speaking of Poland, when he says she 'is poor and depopulated because she confines her industry to agriculture, though she might be at the same time a commercial and manufacturing state.' (I, 13.) And so she might, if she rendered these branches of industry profitable by regulations similar to those by which the governments of Great Britain and France have established them in their respective nations; but she cannot possess commerce and manufactures by any other means.

Public regulations to restrain the importation of certain foreign fabrics, for the purpose of inducing to the manufacture of similar fabrics at home, open thereby to the general industry of the country a much more extensive and more productive employment than they before possessed.

These regulations, by inducing to the establishment of manufacture in the nation, cause much additional labor to be brought into action. And this additional labor, by the aid which it receives from the powers of nature, machinery, and skill, is rendered in the highest degree operative in the multiplication of valuable products.

The great addition, which these products make, to the general circulating capital, occasions an additional employment of labor in the mechanic arts and agriculture. For to the amount which manufacture adds by its products to the general capital, there will be to that amount more to be given in exchange for the product of these other branches. In this general increase of the products of labor, commerce, both foreign and internal, has additional employment for its industry and capital in their distribution.

It is from the productive industry of the nation, that every individual, of which it is composed, derives, either directly or indirectly, his support, income, and wealth.

In proportion as the general industry is increased and rendered more productive by the introduction and establishment of manufacture, in that proportion will be augmented the income of those, who live by the income from fixed capital, by the interest of circulating capital, by the profits on the employment of both, by the salaries of skill, and by the wages of labor.

In this general augmentation of income from capital, skill, and labor productively employed, the general fund is augmented, from which is drawn the incomes of those, who live by their knowledge and talents usefully employed in the public service, and of those also, who live by the exercise of all the other various talents and faculties required and called for in the organization and composition of civilized society. And the incomes of these will naturally increase with the augmentation of the general fund, from which knowledge, talents, and faculties usefully employed draw their compensation.

With respect to those, who live upon fixed incomes from public funds or annuities, their interest is different from the interest of those, who live by their industry, and abilities usefully employed in the service of the community. The incomes of the latter class are increased with the increase of public prosperity, whereas no state of things is so favorable to the fundholder and annuitant as that in which the industry and wealth of the country are declining. This lowers the rents of lands and buildings, and the interest of capital, and the aggregate profits of its employments. It lowers also the wages of labor, and the prices of its products. Hence it is that the fixed incomes in money of the fundholder and annuitant will, when national industry and wealth are declining, command more for them of every thing produced by home industry, which they want or desire, than it would do were the industry and wealth of the country increasing. For when these are increasing, all things, which are the produce of home industry, will be more valuable in relation to money and other foreign commodities, while, in respect of each other, their rise of price being equal, their relative values will remain unchanged.

Therefore Say's arguments, drawn from this source, against regulations for the encouragement of industry, are, on the contrary, good arguments to show their beneficial result. (*B.* I, *ch.* 17.)

For if, in consequence of these regulations, the money, in which the fixed incomes of the fundholder and annuitant consist, commands less of every thing, produced by the labor and talents of the other classes, the fact affords a proof that these other classes, which constitute the great mass of the nation, can command for the employment of their labor and talents a greater compensation or reward, than they would have been able to do without these regulations. Their result thus appears to be, that by increasing the rewards of talents and labor usefully employed, they increase the general industry, and by the increase of that they increase the national wealth.

It is not true that a people will become more industrious, and their industry more productive, in proportion as government leaves industry more to depend upon itself. If it were true, the Indian tribes of America would become the most industrious, and consequently the most wealthy, of people.

Industry requires to be stimulated by rewards; and the industry of a nation will be more active in proportion to the profits which it affords. And the wealth of the nation will advance in proportion to the activity of its industry, and to the degree in which by skill its industry is rendered productive.

Whether the industry of a nation be active or inactive depends upon the government. One portion of the people possesses the capital; the other, and the greater portion, performs the labor. And unless the government, by regulations, render it more profitable to those who possess the capital to employ labor with it at home than it would be to employ labor with it abroad, they will use their capital to maintain foreign industry, and leave that of their own country unemployed, to the impoverishment of the great mass of the people.

By the encouragement of home industry instead of foreign, the producer and consumer are brought nearer to each other, and the great expenses of distant transportation are saved between them to their mutual advantage. This leads at once to an increased production, and an increased consumption; for competition among producers necessarily lowers the price of the product in proportion to the saving of expense in transportation, and people consume more in proportion as they can buy more with the same money.

22. It has been already noticed that the conclusions of Say, as to the effect of government protection to manufacturing industry, when drawn from the actual observation of the beneficial results of it in France, were very different from the conclusions of his general theory. Observation, in the one case, presented to him facts; theory, in the other, led him into error.

The following is another instance of the difference between the results of Say's observation and his theory. In speaking of the want of manufacturing towns in the interior of France for the promotion of its agriculture, he asks, 'What is there but manufactures to give in exchange for agricultural produce?'—and goes on to remark, that 'There are many of the provinces of France, that are miserable enough at present, yet want nothing but towns to bring them into high cultivation. Their situation would, indeed, be hopeless, were we to adopt the system of that class of economists, which recommends the purchase of manufactures from foreign countries, with the raw produce of domestic agriculture.' (II, 154.)

23. Mr. Say argues in favor of government's regulating and controlling the commerce in corn. He says, 'It is unsafe to leave wholly to the providence of individuals the care of supplying an article of such absolute necessity;' and recommends that government should 'fix beforehand a maximum of price, beyond which exportation of grain should either be prohibited, or subjected to heavy duties.' (I, 190, 201.)

Of all restraints, there is none, which has proved so injurious to individual and national interest, as that imposed on the free disposal and *export* of the greatest object of human industry and consumption, corn. Experience has abundantly proved that all interference of governments for its supply is superfluous. Indeed there ought not to be any restraint whatsoever upon the free disposal and export of any one of the products of human industry.

24. Say, in speaking of government's employing labor in productive operations, says 'The annual loss to the nation is the whole excess of the annual consumption of the concern, including wages, which are one item of consumption, above the annual product.' (I, 206.) This is not correct. The nation, on the contrary, is a gainer to the amount of the annual product.

The labor of no country is fully employed, and a country must support its inhabitants, whether it employs them or not; and it costs no more to support them whilst employed, than it does to support them whilst idle.

To employ, therefore, any given number of hands in any new undertaking or improvement on public or private account, though it might in the first instance take those, who were fully employed before, yet as the taking them would leave room for the employment of others to an equal number, who would otherwise have been idle, the whole value of their labor, be it more or less, is to the amount of it, so much clear gain to the country.

The general consumption is not increased by their employment, nor the general capital reduced by their wages. The money paid them for wages is not consumed. It merely changes hands, and the country remains with all the wealth it would have possessed had they not been so employed, together with the value of the labor, which their employment has thus added to it.

The fallacy of Say's reasoning consists in his supposing

all the labor of the nation to be fully employed, and that to employ it in this way prevents the employment of so much labor in a more productive manner. This is not the fact. Labor is nowhere fully employed; and to employ a portion of it in this way actually increases the employment of labor in the other modes, which he supposes to be more profitable. It increases employment, because, to the whole amount of what is produced in this way, there will be, to that amount, so much more to be given in exchange for the products of the labor employed in the other modes.

25. Say observes that, 'Of all the means by which a government can stimulate production, there e so powerful as the perfect security of person and property, especially from the aggressions of arbitrary power;' (I, 209.) and again: 'Survey Europe; and though she is still far short of the prosperity she might attain, most of her kingdoms are in a thriving condition, in spite of taxes and restrictions innumerable, for the simple reason that person and property are there pretty generally safe from violence and arbitrary exaction.' (I, 210.)

If security to person and property be the most powerful means, by which governments can stimulate production, how happens it then that in Europe, where every nation affords that security, those nations, which have most restrained the importation of foreign products, to encourage production at home, should, 'in spite of taxes and restrictions innumerable,' be the most thriving, prosperous, and wealthy; for example, Great Britain and France; while on the other hand that Denmark, and Poland, Spain, and Portugal, nations, which have least restrained the importation of the products of foreign industry, and left their own industry free to employ itself as it could, should be in the most impoverished condition?

26. He says that, 'If the vintage be twice as productive one year as it is in another year, the price of wine falls to half what it was the year preceding.' (I, 269.) This is not correct.

The variations of price do not follow in any such proportion the variations of quantity. The price will be greater or less than this, according to the want or demand there may be for the article.

27. Adam Smith, in his Wealth of Nations, underrating the influence, which habit has to render a man diligent in employment, and which practice has to render him expert, dexterous, and skilful in the application and direction of his labor, objects to the common term of apprenticeships. Say adopts his notions, and quotes his opinion, that 'To teach any young man in the completest manner how to apply the instruments and how to construct the machines of the common mechanic trades, cannot well require the lessons of more than a few weeks, perhaps those of a few days might be sufficient!' and then observes himself, that 'Perhaps there is no mechanic art nearly so difficult as that of the gardener or field laborer!' (I, 174.) As if to build a house, construct a ship, or make a watch, was not 'nearly so difficult,' as to sow a bed of carrots or to reap a field of wheat! But so blind is zeal in support of its theory.

28. Speaking of the bank of England, Say says, 'It must not be imagined that the paper money of that country derives its value from the promise of payment in specie, which it purports to convey;' and further, 'That this paper has a peculiar and inherent value.' (I, 247, 248.)

It is true, however, notwithstanding Say tells us not to imagine it, that the paper money of Great Britain derives its value from the promise of payment in specie, which the bills contain. For neither the paper of the Bank of England, nor that of any other bank, possesses any other value than that which depends on the degree of credit, which the public gives to the punctual performance of the promise.

When a bank suspends payment, as did the Bank of England, its credit is impaired, and the depreciation of its bills is in proportion to the period, to which it is expected the suspension will be continued.

If the suspension proceeds from causes, which it is seen are temporary, the depreciation will be small; but if from causes, which appear to be permanent, the bills will lose their value altogether.

And when he attributes the depreciation, caused by the suspension of specie payments by the Bank of England, merely to the enlargement of the amount of its paper in circulation; and when he says that this depreciation, was only a diminution in value, just like that of any other commodity of inherent value, (I, 248,) he is evidently in great error. For let the amount issued by a bank be ever so great, so long as it continues, according to its promise, to pay specie for its bills, its paper can never depreciate.

29. Say having, as he says, analyzed revenue, though in a manner not very comprehensible, comes to this conclusion. 'The value of revenue is large in proportion not to the value, but to the quantity of the product obtained, to the sum-total of utility created. * * Thus we find that the ratio of national revenue is determined by the amount of the product and not by its value.' (II, 18.)

This is not true. We know by experience that the same quantity of products exported at one time produces, in return, double as much value as when exported at another time. The position applies only to a nation, if there be any such, which consumes all its own products, and exchanges nothing with any oth e.

30. Say observes: 'This will serve to confirm and explain a maxim, which has been hitherto imperfectly understood, and even disputed by many writers and sects of political reasoners, namely, that a country is rich and plentiful, in proportion as the price of commodities is low.' (II, 31.)

This proposition is too general. If the low price of the products of labor is caused by the low wages of labor, it is every where an evidence of the poverty of the great body of people. The high price, on the contrary, is an evidence of the general affluence and increasing wealth and prosperity. The first condition is favorable only to the drones of society, those who live on the labor of others; the latter is promotive of the prosperity of all the productive and useful classes, the great mass of the community.

In nations, which are advancing in wealth and population, the wages of labor and the price of the products of labor are higher than in those nations, which are stationary or declining. A rise in the price of products augments the profits of industry, and causes more labor to be employed. This increases production, and, with production, wealth.

31. Say says, that 'A full grown man is an accumulated capital.' (II, 75, *note.*)

The prodigal, if full grown, is then an accumulated capital. Say considers capital one of the sources of production. Prodigality must, then, according to him, be capital productively employed. Capital he also calls an agent of production. In that case, the prodigality of a full grown man must be the productive agency of capital!

32. 'It has been sometimes supposed,' he says, 'that capital is multiplied by the operation of credit. This error, though frequently recurring in books professing to treat of political economy, can only arise from a total ignorance of the nature and functions of capital.' (II, 102.)

It is not an error to suppose that capital is multiplied by credit. Money is a component part of capital. Credit performs the functions of money to a considerable extent, and the effect is the same as though capital had been increased to that extent.

33. Say considers that 'The portion of capital embarked in domestic agriculture is employed best for the interest of the nation.' (I, 112.)

That portion of capital is employed most to the interest of the nation, which is employed with the greatest profit, and which, in proportion to its amount, employs the greatest quantity of labor, and at the same time affords to the labor it employs the greatest remuneration,—no matter in whatever branch of industry.

34. Say observes that 'All the commodities, which a nation imports, must be reckoned as part of its annual product, and all its exports as part of its annual consumption.'(II, 161.)

These propositions are mere absurdities. The imports of a nation are purchased with that portion of its products, which is beyond its own consumption. Of its imports thus purchased, one part is consumed, another is retained for use, and a part is in money, which goes towards the accumulation of capital.

35. Say considers the internal commerce of a country to be more advantageous than the foreign. (I, 62.) The American editor of his work thinks Say has fallen into an error here, in common with Adam Smith, and makes some remarks in his note, which are correct so far as they relate to the profit on the employment of equal amounts of commercial capital, but which do not prove that Say entertains an erroneous opinion upon this point.

It is not solely by the profit on the commercial capital employed, that a nation derives advantage from its commerce. It derives an advantage, likewise, from the profit on production to which its commerce encourages.

In our foreign commerce, though we have the whole profit on the capital employed, yet we share or divide with foreign nations the profits upon production, to which it gives rise. Whereas in our home-commerce, while we have the same profit on an equal amount of capital employed, we have double the profit on the home-production, to which it encourages, in every exchange it makes of home-products. For it encourages to double the production, which the foreign commerce does. And in proportion as these exchanges are made in less time and at less expense between us at home, than they can be made between us and foreign nations, in that proportion is the home-commerce still more advantageous to us than is our commerce with foreign nations.

36. Speaking of the state of agricultural industry in France,

Say observes: 'There are many of the provinces of France, that are miserable enough at present. Their situation would indeed be hopeless, were we to adopt the system of that class of economists, which recommends the purchase of manufactures from foreign countries with the raw produce of domestic agriculture.' (II, 154.)

This sound conclusion of Say's does not accord, it seems, with the American editor's theory. He observes in opposition to it, in his note upon the passage, that 'A system of policy, which should attempt, by restraints or encouragements, to divert a portion of the capital and industry employed in agriculture or commerce from those channels towards the erection of a town, or the establishmeut of a manufactory, with a view to promote the better cultivation of the soil, would be subversive of this end.'

No government, it is presumable, would ever attempt so foolish a thing,—foolish because impossible,—as to 'divert capital from agriculture,' to the building of a town or the establishment of a manufactory.

It is not by the fixed capital of agriculture, that works of this kind can be executed. It is by the general circulating capital only that it is done. The execution of any such work, instead of diverting capital from agriculture, actually turns capital thither. It gives to the farmer money in exchange for rude materials, and for provisions to supply the workmen employed.

No farmer will object to the opening of a new market for his produce. He does not call the selling this at better prices a diversion of capital from him to his injury. And it is this portion only, by the sale of which the farmer is enriched, which can enter into the building of towns or the establishment of manufactories. The other portion of agricultural capital, consisting of land, live-stock, buildings, and tools, cannot change place.

The incorrectness of the other branch of the editor's proposition, respecting the diversion of capital from commerce, is yet more manifest. Circulating capital and labor will never leave one employment for another, unless this other should be the most profitable : in which case both the capital and labor which remain, as well as those which depart, will have more profitable employment than they had before.

37. The American editor then proceeds to settle with wonderful celerity the long agitated question as to the 'cause' upon which the prosperity and opulence of nations 'depend.' This he does by assuming as a principle, that 'The prosperity of agriculture, as well as that of every other branch of industry, depends upon the unrestrained operation of individual interest;' and that 'All that is necessary to enable a state to reach the highest pitch of opulence, is not to disturb the action of this important principle.' (II, 154, *note.*)

An important principle, to be sure, were it but true ; for in that case we might save all the expense and avoid all the evils arising from the institutions of government and law.

Every individual might then unrestrainedly pursue his own interest, without any regard to the interest of others, and we might reach as high a pitch of opulence thereby, as our neighbors, the Indian tribes, have done, who are so enlightened as 'not to disturb the action of this important principle' by any of the restraints, which the organization of civilized society imposes.

One might well suppose that the American editor could not mean this extensive application of his general principle, were it not that he lays it down and reasons upon it, without limitation or exception.

38. Indeed, he asserts 'There is *no* exception to the general principle, that what is most productive to the individual is so to the community at large.' (II, 115.) Gambling, fraud, violence, may be productive to the individual; but are they so to the community at large ?

The wealth of the community proceeds from productive industry; and it is by regulations, which render it more profitable to those, who possess the capital, to employ labor with it at home, than it would be to employ labor with it abroad, that the industry and wealth of the country are most promoted.

REVIEW

OF

M'CULLOCH'S POLITICAL ECONOMY.

I. SUBJECT AND DEFINITIONS.

THIS work, it appears, is brought before the public, by Mr. M'Vickar, Professor of Political Economy in Columbia College; and since, under such authority, it is likely to go into the hands of students, it demands particular notice.

Mr. M'Vickar informs us, that the author of the article which he has republished, from the Edinburgh supplement to the Encyclopedia Britannica, is J. R. M'Culloch, Esq., the Ricardo Lecturer on Political Economy, in London.

The general theory which it maintains, in reference to the most efficient means of promoting wealth, we think to be erroneous, and that were it reduced to practice, it would prove very detrimental to the interests of a nation; as we shall hope to demonstrate, when we come to examine the peculiar doctrines of the work under their different heads. And as we proceed we shall point out other errors in theory, of less practical importance.

Mr. M'Culloch commences his Essay, by giving a definition of the science, which treats of the nature and causes of the wealth of nations; but instead of giving it in those concise and comprehensive terms of Smith, he defines it in the following objectionable manner. 'Political economy is the science of the laws, which regulate the production, distribution, and consumption, of those material products, which have exchangeable value, and which are either necessary, useful, or agreeable to man.' (7.)

This definition of political economy, in which Mr. M'Culloch also includes his definition of wealth, is liable to the following objections.

1st. It limits the enquiries of political economy to the production, distribution, and consumption of wealth, and thereby excludes from its notice the uses and the accumulation of wealth.

2d. It confines political economy to the consideration of such material products only, as have exchangeable value, and thereby excludes from its investigations a considerable portion of national wealth, which is estimated by its utility, and not by its exchangeable value, namely, that portion, which consists in roads, bridges, public edifices, fortifications, internal improvements, and so forth, denominated collectively public property.

3d. In the definition of wealth, which it includes, it makes no distinction between national and individual wealth. The constituents of one are not, in all cases, the same as those of the other. The amount of national wealth is not, as some persons state it to be, precisely the same as the sum-total of individual wealth. The debt of the nation is, to the individuals, to whom it is due, wealth. But it would be absurd to reckon this portion of individual wealth, as wealth to the nation who owes it.

4th. The latter clause of the definition is altogether superfluous; for whenever a material product possesses exchangeable value, that circumstance alone places it among the constituents of wealth, and as such within the investigations of political economy.

II. FREE TRADE THEORY.

Mr. M'Culloch, in treating of what he calls the principles of the science, and of its history, developes his free-trade-theory, and quotes the opinions of many writers on foreign trade in support of it.

This theory, we shall endeavor to show, is not founded on admitted principles, but on mere assumptions. It is in direct opposition to the practical system of policy pursued by those nations, in which wealth and knowledge have made the most rapid progress.

For instance, it is opposed to the sound policy, which Great Britain pursues, of securing, by legislative enactments, to the products of her own industry, the exclusive benefits of her own markets. A policy which, by assuring to the national industry its natural reward, has afforded it the means of attaining that high pitch of productive power, which is the great source of this nation's overflowing wealth. That it has been the effect of that policy, the history of British industry fully confirms.

Mr. M'Culloch however does not accede to the policy of encouraging industry by legislative enactments. 'The principles,' says he, 'upon which the production and accumulation of wealth, and the progress of civilization depend, are not the offspring of legislative enactments.' (15.) Nobody ever contended, that the inherent principles of our nature were the offspring of legislative enactments; but it does not follow from this, that the development and operation of the principles, upon which the progress of civilization, and the accumulation of wealth depend, are not the offspring of legislative enactments. To advance the above position was merely saying, that those principles of our nature which induce to action, are not the offspring of the acts to which they induce.

The principle, which leads man to the production and accumulation of those things, upon which the support and enjoyment of human life depend, is inherent in his nature; but it is a principle, which, in that state which precedes civilization, does not develope itself in action, beyond the exertions necessary to the support of a mere existence.

It is, however, owing to the influence of this principle on the natural intelligence of man, that no sooner is he able to supply the natural wants of life, than he seeks to possess those things, which are essential to its enjoyment. This endeavor has slowly, though gradually, led to the adoption of all those legislative regulations, upon which the security of property, the progress of civilization, the activity of industry, the increase of production, and the accumulation of wealth, depend.

Mr. M'Culloch next deduces from premises, which authorize no such conclusion, 'That it is sound policy to allow every individual to follow the bent of his inclination, and engage in any branch of industry he thinks proper.' (15.) He does not admit the expediency of his being restrained from those pursuits, which offend against good morals, or which disturb the peace of society, or which are detrimental to the public interest, or which retard the progress of public prosperity; for if he admitted the expediency of restraints in these instances, he would conceive at once the propriety and policy of those restrictions against which he so zealously contends.

The premises, from which he has drawn the above untenable position, will appear in the following quotation. 'It is an admitted principle in the science of morals, as well as of political economy, that by far the largest proportion of the human race have a much clearer view of what is conducive to their own interests, than it is possible for any other man or select number of men to have; and consequently that it is sound policy to allow every individual to follow the bent of his inclination, and engage in any branch of industry he thinks proper.' (15.) The absurdity of the conclusion, that because men are the best judges of their own interests, therefore they ought to be allowed to pursue them, without any regard to the interests of others, or to the public interest, will be readily perceived. This conclusion, however, Mr. M'Culloch terms, by way of distinction, 'the general theorem,' and this is one of the fundamental principles of his free-trade theory.

We shall now show that the foregoing premises, from which Mr. M'Culloch deduces in so strange a way his general theorem, lead to a conclusion directly the reverse of it, which is, that the interests of the few ought to be subordinate to the interests of the many.

It is an alleged principle in legislation, that men are the best judges of their own interest. Therefore, when the agriculturists, the mechanics, the manufacturers, and the merchants, the productive classes of a nation, and composing by far the largest portion of its inhabitants, come forward, as they have done in this and other countries, separately, and unite in stating to the government, that it would be conducive to their respective interests, to be secured against foreign competition in the home-markets and home-trade by restrictive regulations, the government must, upon the foregoing principle, that men are the best judges of their own interests, admit that such regulations would conduce to the interests of by far the largest portion of the nation. Now, as it is the duty of government to consult the interests of the greatest number, it becomes obligatory on them to establish the restrictive regulations, which it is thus proved to them would promote the interests of the greatest number, or in other words promote the interest of the nation.

Having established the conclusion, that the interests of the greatest number require that foreign importation should be subject to modified restrictions, it necessarily follows that, without such restrictions, the interests of the individual would, in the importation of foreign commodities, in some instances, be opposed to the interests of the public, and therefore that he ought, in such instances, to be subject to restrictive regulations.

'Foreign trade, between different and independent countries,' observes Mr. M'Culloch, 'will contribute to increase the wealth of each, in precisely the same manner, that the trade between different provinces of the same kingdom contributes to increase their wealth.' (68.) And again, 'When the freedom of commerce is not restricted, each country necessarily devotes itself to such employments as are most beneficial to each.' (69.)

The interest of the individual in a state of society is of a two-fold nature. He has, besides his private interest, a share in the public interest. To the first he is sufficiently sensible. To the latter his attention is rarely drawn, unless it be at those times when, by public regulations, industry has been suddenly stimulated to greatly augment its powers of production, as was recently the case in the United States. Then it is, that the working classes perceive, that there is not only a greater demand for their labor, but that they are able to draw from the accumulating stock of general wealth, a proportionately greater share than they did before, in remuneration for the same quantity of labor.

As the public interest is under the safeguard of government, whose duty it is to protect and cherish it, the individual looks chiefly to the proportion of his private interest. This, the individual, in respect to the *internal* industry and trade of the nation, ought to be allowed to pursue, in any way he may think most beneficial to himself, subject only to such limitations and restrictions, as arise from moral considerations. But, in regard to foreign commerce, he ought always to be subject to such limitations and restrictions, as not only the public morals require, but such, also, as the public policy and the national interest may require.

There are many political economists, who, like Mr. M'Culloch, from observing the benefits which the individuals of a community derived from a free interchange of the products of their industry among themselves, have been, by generalizing without sufficient discrimination, led into the error of supposing that the same freedom of interchange between nations would be equally advantageous to them. The two cases are totally different, for, between the members of a community, the establishment of a free-trade is practicable, but, between nations, it is impracticable.

In one case the establishment of it is beneficial; in the other, were it possible to establish it, the establishment of it would be prejudicial to the nation at large, although it might be beneficial to the particular communities or individuals, in whose favor it was established.

In a nation there is a *sovereign power* to protect individuals in the free interchange of the products of their industry among themselves, and a *public interest* to render this free interchange equally beneficial to them. But, among nations, there is neither a *general controlling power* to establish a free interchange between them, nor a *public interest*, to render it advantageous to them, if it could be established.

In a community, when the employment of capital is confined to *internal* industry, the more capital an individual employs, the more he promotes the industry and prosperity of every other individual.

And the more the capital of an individual is increased by its employment, in this way, the more it conduces to increase the employment of labor, and the consequent wealth of the community.

But the employment of capital in foreign-trade, is not always, as it is in internal trade, promotive of the prosperity of the community. It is not, for instance, in the importation of such foreign commodities, as could, with equal skill, be produced at home with as little labor as they are produced with abroad. And the more capital an individual employs in this branch of foreign trade, the more he lessens the employment of labor at home, and the greater is the loss to the community. For, though the importation of the commodities afford the individual a profit on his capital, yet it causes a loss to the community of more than ten times as much, by preventing the home production of them.

Hence, to infer that because an unrestricted *internal* trade is beneficial to a nation, therefore an unrestricted foreign trade must be equally so too, is to come to an unwarranted and false conclusion. Among the individuals of a community, the wealth of one is conducive to the interest of all. Not so, among nations. With them wealth is power, and the power of one will ever be opposed to the power of others. Each nation will strive to augment its own wealth and power, and oppose the like endeavor in other nations.

Every nation will still continue to impose duties on foreign imports, either for revenue, or for the encouragement of internal industry; and whether it be for one or the other, they will alike operate as restrictions on the freedom of intercourse between them.

But were it possible for all nations to agree together, to abolish duties on imports and exports, and to do away with every restriction on the interchange of commodities one with another, and thus give application to the theoretical system in practice, the operation of it would be to increase foreign intercourse, and cause more capital and labor to be employed in transportation,—to diminish the industry, wealth, and population of the more opulent nations, and increase the industry, wealth, and population of the poorer nations.

And though it might enlarge the aggregate amount of production, yet the aggregate would have been greater, had they all adopted the practical system of regulating foreign intercourse, according to their different conditions, and as their respective interests might have required. If each nation adopted measures, for producing within itself, so far as its natural capabilities advantageously admitted, every commodity which it required for its own use and consumption, it would, by thus placing the producer and consumer side by side together, release much capital and labor from the business of transportation, to be employed in production. And each nation would thus, besides what it saved in reducing its transportation, be a great gainer by the increase of its production.

We have observed above, that the effect of abolishing all restrictions on foreign trade, would be to render the rich nations poorer, and the poor nations richer; but as this perhaps may not be admitted by all, we shall endeavor to demonstrate it.

To this end therefore, we will suppose a free-trade to be opened between Great Britain and Poland. In this case, Great Britain would import corn from Poland, because she could import it cheaper than she raises it. This, it is evident, would diminish agricultural production in England and increase it in Poland. And by diminishing it in England, it would cause a decrease of production in every other branch of her industry. For whatever reduces production in one branch, excepting excess of supply, reduces, to the amount of it, the means of an effective demand for the products of the other branches; since there will be to that amount less produced to purchase them with.

But it will be objected here, that what these other classes thus lose on the one hand, by the reduced means of the agricultural class of their own country, they will gain on the other by the increased means of the agricultural class in Poland. To this we answer, that the means of both classes together, even were Poland to expend the whole of hers in England, would fall short of those, which the agricultural class of England alone before employed to the benefit of the other classes of British industry. For though the quantity of corn drawn from both sources for the supply of the British market, should be greater now than it was before, yet its aggregate value would be less.

Now, when we add to this, that Poland would probably

lay out the greater portion of what Great Britain might pay her for corn, in the products of other climates and other countries, instead of expending it in England for the employment and support of her industry, it must be clear, that the reduced demand for British products would diminish production, in a greater or less degree, in every department of British industry.

But it is not only in production that Great Britain would lose, she would lose also in transportation. Northern ships are navigated cheaper than British; they would, consequently, soon crowd the British ships out of employment.

That it costs Great Britain more to raise corn and carry on navigation, than it does some other nations, is to be ascribed in part to her restrictive regulations. And it is to the effect which these have, in increasing the cost of production and transportation, that the great clamor and outcry against them is owing.

This effect, however, which the opposers of these regulations adduce as a proof of their injurious consequences, affords the best evidence of their beneficial operation. For the increased cost of production does not arise from there being more capital and labor expended in the same quantity of products; there is less. But it arises from these regulations securing, to the employment of capital *greater benefits*, and to labor *greater wages:* the two circumstances upon which the rapid progress of national wealth depends. Now as these restrictions on foreign trade have the effect to raise wages, the removal of them would consequently have the effect to lower wages. Indeed, the removal of them, and the adoption of the free-trade system in their place, would have that effect; and would thus leave the home-laborer without employment, or force him to work as cheaply, and live as miserably, as the poor peasantry are obliged to do, of the foreign country with which the free trade might be opened.

Such, therefore, being the necessary result of this system, Great Britain might, undoubtedly, attain at length to that enviable condition, to which her political economists would lead her: a condition in which she would, by the reduction of profits and wages, be very likely to raise corn, and sail ships, as cheaply as the poorest of the nations, which have had the theoretical wisdom to leave their foreign trade most free from restrictive regulations.

Without however entering into a detail of all the consequences, which would result from the adoption of the free-trade theory in practice, it is sufficient, to the end we proposed, to show, as in the case between England and Poland, that production would be diminished by it in England, and increased by it in Poland. For, as production is the effect of industry, and the cause of wealth and population, we think that, in showing its diminution in the case of England, and its increase in the case of Poland, we establish the position, that a free-trade between nations would diminish the industry, wealth, and population of the richer nations, and increase the industry, wealth, and population of the poorer nations. Now, unless Great Britain would force a portion of her lands out of cultivation, and a portion of her laborers out of employment; unless she would reduce her working classes, to live on as miserable a pittance as the northern peasantry are constrained to do; unless she would lower rents, profits, and wages, and thus diminish the sources of national revenue; unless she would lower the value of real estate, and lessen the quantity of personal:—in short, unless she would, from that pre-eminence of wealth and power, to which she has arisen under the sound practical system of policy pursued by her statesmen, descend to an equality of condition with the poorer nations, she will not abandon the only system, which has the sanction of experience, to adopt the leveling, theoretical, and improved system contended for by certain political economists.

No nation, indeed, can ever have an interest in importing from another any commodities, which it has equal natural capabilities of producing within itself. Capital and skill are never wanting, where an adequate profit on their employment is secured; and this security the government always has it in its power to afford, by the mere regulation of duties on imports.

New branches of industry, thus established, soon produce their various commodities, as cheaply as similar ones were produced in the nation from which they were before imported. The producers are brought nearer to the consumers, and the expenses of a distant transportation are saved. Production is increased, not only by what the new branches of industry add to it, but also by the increase of production to which that addition gives rise in every previous branch; for, in the products of the former, there is so much more to be given in exchange for the products of the latter.

The interest, which every nation thus clearly has, in multiplying the sources of wealth within itself, by a modified restriction of the import of certain foreign commodities, will, independently of the considerations before offered, prevent the theory of free and unrestricted commerce between nations from ever being adopted by them in practice.

It appears, therefore, that the same general principles, which are applicable to the *internal trade* of a nation, are inapplicable to its *foreign*, and that the same freedom of interchange, which is beneficial in the former case, would, in the latter, be prejudicial.

And the difference between the operation of the practical system, in regulating foreign-trade, and the theoretical system, of letting it alone, may be shewn by numerical calculation; proving how much more the former conduces to the interest of a nation, than what the latter would, and that nations would be gainers were each to regulate their foreign intercourse upon the same practical principles.

Let us suppose, for instance, the woollen manufacture of the United States to be sustained by a duty of 25 per cent on foreign woollens, that it produces annually goods to the value of $9,000,000, and that the cost of producing them is made up of the following items:

1st. Raw materials, including 5,000,000 lbs. wool, - - - - - - - -	$3,000,000
2d. Wages of labor, and interest of fixed capital,	5,181,819
	8,181,819
3d. Manufacturers' profit on circulating capital employed, 10 per cent. - - - -	818,181
	$9,000,000

While foreign woollens continue to be imported, it is their cost, including duty, which regulates the price of the American. Now suppose the duty to be abolished, and that the merchant in consequence imports a like amount; for in this case he could import them cheaper than the American manufacturer could make them.

Therefore, as their assumed cost, with the duty on, including profits, is - - - - - - - $9,000,000
and the duty on them would have been, say 1,812,500

they would, with this duty off, cost to import them, including profits, - - - - -	7,187,500

And the cost of importing them would be made up of the following items:

1st. Cost in the foreign country - -	$6,434,091
2d. Freight, which pays the profits on all the capital, and the wages of all the labor, employed in ship-building and navigation - - -	100,000
	6,534,091
3d. Merchants' profit on capital employed in the two foregoing items, 10 per cent. - -	653,409
	$7,187,500

From which it appears that the gain to the country on the manufacture of these goods, in the profits on capital, and the wages of labor, is -	$6,000,000
And that the gain to the country, on their importation, in the profits on capital and the wages of labor, would be - - - - -	753,409
Now deduct one from the other, and it leaves	$5,246,591

From which it further appears, that the gain to the country is $5,246,591 more on their manufacture, than it would have been on their importation, and that consequently it would lose to that amount annually, were it to repeal the duty, and substitute the importation of them, for their home production.

Besides, the fixed capital of the manufacture, which is more productive, would in that case become useless, and its value be almost totally lost.

Further, the manufacturing laborers, who would be thrown out of employment, would, instead of being, as they now are, profitable consumers of the products of those engaged in other branches of industry, become sharers with these in their diminished profits to the equal loss of the whole.

But the loss would not be limited here; the farmer would partake of it. Wool is not an article of exportation from this country. Its present high prices depend upon the demand for the home-manufacture. Let the home-manufacture be done away with, by foreign importation, and the demand for wool would cease, the prices of it would sink, and the production of it be diminished.

If it be objected to this, that our increased importation of foreign cloths would increase the foreign demand for wool, we answer, that this would rather tend to increase the growth of wool abroad, than to cause the exportation of it from this country; for unless, by the cessation of the home-manufacture, the prices of it were greatly reduced, it could not be exported; and in either case a loss must be sustained upon it.

The ship-owner would also be a loser; for by the additional investment abroad in goods of little bulk, of upwards of six millions of dollars, which the repeal of the duty would cause, there would be to that amount less of the proceeds of our exports to be invested in articles of greater bulk, wherein otherwise that amount would be invested. He, therefore, by the loss of the bulky freight which this must cause, would lose probably five times as much as he would gain by the freight of the woollens.

The mercantile class would be still greater losers; for, in the discontinuance of this branch of industry by the repeal of the duty, nine millions of dollars less in value would be produced in the country, to be distributed by them in the internal trade. And there would not, on the other hand, from that cause, be any additional employment for their capital in foreign commerce. Their importations would be to the same amount as before; the objects of investment only would be changed; more manufactured goods would come, and as much less of other articles, which would have paid a better freight.

The demand of foreign nations for our products would be none the greater because of our importing more woollens, and therefore our export for the supply of those nations would not be enlarged. Now as the proceeds of the exports regulate the amount of the imports, and as the exports would not be increased, it is clear there would be no increase in the amount of our imports; and therefore that there could not, in consequence of the repeal of the duty, be any more capital employed in foreign commerce; and we have already seen that this repeal would cause much less capital to be employed in the internal commerce.

In short, the nation at large would sustain a loss of near nine millions of dollars annually, for there would be a diminution to that amount in home production, and no increase in the aggregate amount of our foreign importation.

III. CAPITAL IN RELATION TO LABOR.

We now proceed to examine Mr. M'Culloch's doctrine on the subject of capital, and point out those errors, which, by entering into his general reasonings, have concurred to lead him to his incorrect conclusions, touching the causes upon which the increase and accumulation of national wealth depend. These errors principally arise from his confounding cause and effect, and from his ascribing to a single cause, what several have concurred to produce. 'The division of labor,' he says, 'is a consequence of the previous accumulation of capital.' (78.) We should rather suppose, on the contrary, the accumulation of capital to be the consequence of a division of labor. The division of labor has its origin in the natural differences there are between men. One has more strength, another more ingenuity. The one is led by his physical capabilities to one kind of employment, the other by his mental faculties to a different one. The power of individuals, thus to choose their employment, does not depend on any extraordinary accumulation of capital. For as the ordinary means, which every family possesses, for subsisting its several members, are sufficient to enable each to apply their labor, according to their different capacities and inclinations, in the way most conducive to the supply of their common wants,—so are the ordinary means, which every nation possesses, for subsisting its inhabitants, sufficient to enable each individual to direct his labor in the way most advantageous to himself, and consequently to admit of a division of labor to any degree in which it may be found profitable.

Thus, while an agricultural population is thin and scattered, as for instance in the back settlements of the United States, the division of labor is confined chiefly to the members of a family. It is not so confined, however, because the various articles of support are no where laid up in a sufficient abundance to extend it beyond, but because its further extension would be of no advantage to the parties. But as their population increases and becomes more dense, the mechanic arts and commerce gradually arise, and the division of occupation is extended, as far as it is found to be individually advantageous. It is not, however, until the introduction and establishment of manufacture in a nation, through public measures adapted to that purpose, that the division of labor receives its greatest extension. And then it is, that we see how greatly this division of labor, together with the powers of nature brought into action in manufacture, co-operate to accelerate the production, and consequently the accumulation, of wealth in a nation.

Again, under the same head, Mr. M'Culloch states that, 'As the accumulation of stock must have preceded the division of labor, so its subsequent division can only be extended, as capital is more and more accumulated.' (78.) On the contrary, it is from the previous division of labor, which renders industry more productive, that the excess of the annual production over the annual consumption arises, and consequently, this excess, in which the accumulation of wealth consists, cannot precede the division of labor, which is the cause of it.

Mr. M'Culloch, still continuing to substitute effect for cause in his reasoning, goes on to state, that, without a previous increase of capital, machinery cannot be improved, nor the productive powers of labor augmented. (83.) Now if we ask how capital can be increased, without previously employing more labor or increasing the productive powers of that already employed?—we are answered, by parsimony. On this point Mr. M'Culloch has adopted the theory of Adam Smith, that the increase of wealth is owing to economy, and not to industry. This theory has been disputed, and the dispute has been called an idle one, (note, 85,) because industry and economy are both necessary to wealth. This is very true, in reference to individual wealth; but the increase of national wealth does not depend upon the greater economy of the individual; it depends upon the increase of production.

The profusion of some individuals, by which they impoverish themselves, is a gain to others, by which they enrich themselves, and the state is none the poorer for it. On the contrary, by property thus passing from the hands of the idle and profuse, to those of the industrious and frugal, the state may be benefited by it.

Now the question, whether national wealth depends on individual industry or on individual economy, is neither a speculative nor an idle one. It is an important question, a question upon which governments have had different opinions, and which difference of opinion has led to very different practical results.

From the adoption of the erroneous doctrine, that the increase of national wealth depends on individual economy, and not on individual industry, have resulted sumptuary enactments, or laws to restrain individual expenditure, and at the same time, a total neglect of encouragement to productive industry. But from the opposite and the correct opinion, that the increase of national wealth depends on the increase of the power of productive industry, and not on individual economy, the practical result has been, to leave individuals to regulate their expenses according to their pleasure, as a matter of no consequence to the state; and to establish such regulations as would call into action the greatest quantity of labor, and render that labor at the same time in the greatest degree productive. In a nation, where the *economical* doctrine should be the governing principle, the people at large would be in a state of poverty, and remain so; for as the profits of capital and the wages of labour would be low, the laborer could not, by his daily exertions, do more, than just supply himself with what was necessary to his daily consumption; and from this, economy could extract nothing to go towards the accumulation of wealth.

But in a nation, where the productive power of its industry is held to be the source of its accumulating wealth, and where, consequently, it is held to be sound policy to uphold, cherish, and protect it, there the people will be found to be in a flourishing condition. For, as the profits of capital and the wages of labor will be high, none will want employment, and, from the ample renumeration of industry, all will be able to lay by something as a future resource. And thus, the more the people are able to accumulate, the more will their desire to accumulate increase, and this, while it will animate them to increased industry, will lead them to the practice of greater comparative economy.

Economy proceeds from the desire, which is natural to man, of improving his condition, and rising in the world ; it consequently operates with great uniformity, in its general effects. What it saves from income to add to capital, is in constant proportion to the means that industry supplies it with, out of which to make a saving.

Industry, on the contrary, is as valuable in its operations, as economy is uniform in its results. Industry depends for its support, and for the energy of its action, upon the remuneration it derives from profits. Profits are increased or diminished by an infinite variety of circumstances, which operate on them, and industry is increased and diminished with them.

Mr. M'Culloch is obliged to assume, for the support of his theory on this subject, that the labor of a nation is generally as fully employed as its means will permit ;—an assumption contradicted by uniform experience. The laborers of no nation are ever so fully employed, as they would be, were the profits on their employment greater. It is not for the want of means, but for the want of inducements to use those means, that more labor is not employed.

'The produce of the labor of a nation,' says Mr. M'Culloch, 'cannot be increased otherwise than by an increase in the number of laborers, or by an increase in the productive powers of the existing laborers. But without an increase of capital, it is in most cases impossible to employ another workman with advantage.' (82) Again, 'When no additions are made to the stock of a country, no more labor will be, or indeed can be, employed.' (84.) Further, 'It is impossible that the demand for labor can be increased, without an increase of capital.' (171.) These propositions are all evidently at variance with facts within every one's observation.

In every nation, there are times, when more laborers are employed than at other times, not because there is more or less capital, at these different times, but because there is more profit on the employment of labor with capital, at one time, than at another. Nothing, indeed, can be more devoid of truth than the assumption, that without a previous addition to capital, no additional labor can be employed in a nation; an assumption necessary, however, though devoid of truth, to enable Mr. M'Culloch to arrive at the conclusion to which he aims, namely, that as no additional labor can be employed in a country, without a previous increase of capital, no country can possibly, by any measures it may adopt, increase the number of its productive laborers, and consequently, that the best a government can do, is to let the protection and encouragement of industry alone. A reference to our own experience, will show clearly, how utterly unfounded is this doctrine of Mr. M'Culloch's.

The United States, in 1816, adopted measures to increase production, by rendering it more profitable to employ labor in manufacturing industry, than it was before. This had the effect to bring into action a great number of additional laborers. Production was augmented in the manufacturing branch of industry, and this caused the increase of production in every other branch; for, to the amount of the additional product in the manufacturing branch, there was, to that amount, so much more to be given in exchange for the products of the other branches. Thus, by the general increase of productive industry, the general wealth of the country has been greatly augmented; not however by diminishing consumption, but by increasing production; not by a previous augmentation of capital through the savings of economy, but by legislative measures, rendering the employment of labor more profitable to capital, and thus causing the additional employment of labor.

If a nation possesses the means of subsisting its inhabitants, which every nation is assumed to do, it also possesses the means of affording them full employment; for it is in the means of subsistence, food, and clothing, that the means of employment consist. Therefore, if the inhabitants of any nation, whose laws afford ample security to property, as the laws of most civilized nations do, are generally in a state of indigence through want of employment, it is not because there is not sufficient capital for their employment, but because the employment of them would not be profitable to the holders of capital.

The wealth of a nation consists in its land, and in the material products of its industry. Its capital consists in that portion of wealth, which is employed for purposes of income or profit. Now public regulations, which increase the profits of capital employed in domestic industry, cause more wealth to be employed as capital, and cause more labor to be called into action for its employment. And the more wealth there is brought into action as capital, and of labor for its employment, the greater will be the aggregate income from labor and capital, and the faster will the national wealth augment.

It is owing to the high profits, which it has been the policy of Great Britain to secure to capital in every department of her industry, that there has been, in that nation, a more extensive employment for capital, and a more full employment for labor, than in any other in Europe. Hence her more rapid increase in wealth and population. And if, instead of her oppressive and unequal laws, which kept down the wages of labor below their natural level, the laborer had been left at liberty to stand out for such wages with his employer as corresponded to the demand for labor, the wealth of the nation would have been more equally distributed, and both its wealth and population would have been still greater.

In the nations of Europe, the land is all appropriated and held by a very small class of their respective inhabitants. Every other kind of property, also, owing to the peculiar organization of civil government in those nations, concentrates itself in comparatively few hands. The working classes therefore, composing the great mass of the people, are there entirely dependant on the property-holders for employment and support.

Whether or not it be, that some political economists, from limiting their views to this state of things, in which laborers are entirely dependant on the capital of others for employment, have fallen into the error of supposing that the employment of labor is in proportion to capital, and that without a previous increase of capital no more labor can be employed, is a question of no importance to determine. It is the practical consequences alone of the error, which we consider.

We have before adverted to the conclusion to which it leads in respect to government, namely, that as no additional labor can be employed, without a previous addition to capital, no government can possibly, by any measures it may adopt, increase the number of its productive laborers, and therefore, that the best it can do, is to let alone the protection and encouragement of industry by restrictive regulations, and 'allow every individual to follow the bent of his inclination, and engage in any branch of industry he thinks proper.' (15.)

Mr. M'Culloch deduces this general rule, it will be remembered, from the principle, that men are the best judges of their own interest; but it follows more logically, from his erroneous assumption as to the relation of capital to labor, than it does from the principle above-mentioned; for from the former it follows as a necessary consequence. This rule in theory makes a delusive show of being equal, just, and liberal. In practice it is the reverse of all this. It is unequal, because, owing to the great inequality of conditions in society, it is a privilege only to a few, to those who possess the capital. It is these only who can avail themselves of it. To the great body of the people, those who live by labor, it is no privilege; they cannot profit by it. Labor cannot, like capital, readily transport itself abroad in search of more profitable employment.

It is unjust, because it leads those, who possess the capital, to employ it in a manner, which is prejudicial to the interest of those from whose labors alone they derived it.

It is illiberal, because it directs the attention solely to self-interest, in disregard of all other interests, and by opening the way to the property-holders to supply some of their wants a little cheaper by the employment of foreign labor, it induces them to overlook the interests of the home-laborers, who are entirely dependant on them for employment; and for the sake of saving sixpence to themselves in the price of a commodity, have recourse to foreign labor, and deprive the home-laborers of an employment, which would have been worth six shillings to them.

And while this rule, which Mr. M'Culloch designates as 'the general theorem,' would operate in a manner so prejudicial to the interests of the laboring classes, the property-holder, in this result of it, would lose in income, by the diminished product of labor at home, a great deal more than he would save by employing cheaper labor abroad. To elucidate this proposition, suppose some circumstance renders the employment of capital, in the different divisions of internal industry, more profitable; as for instance, by the exclusion from the home-market, of such foreign products as can be made or produced at home. The consequence of it would be, to increase the demand for labor. This would raise the rate of wages; more workmen would be taken into employment; and this would increase production. The increase of production would raise the rent of lands, dwelling houses, ware-houses, shops, and in short, the income from every description of real property, to the benefit of the property-holders. The increase of rents, profits, and wages, would increase the demand for all the products of industry. The greater demand would still further augment production, and a more rapid increase of wealth would be the general result.

Now let us suppose, on the contrary, the home-markets to be thrown open to the free admission, without duty, of all foreign products. The consequence of it would be to lessen the demand for domestic products. This would reduce their price. The fall of price would lower the profits on capital employed in their production. This would lessen the demand for labor, lower the rate of wages, and throw out of employment many laborers. With the reduction of labor, production would be diminished, and this would reduce the quantity of circulating capital. The reduction of circulating capital would lower the income of fixed capital, or of every kind of real property, and in lowering its income it would diminish its exchangeable value.

Thus it appears, that while the property-holders would save a little in the price of a commodity by its free importation, they would lose incalculably more, by the diminished home-production which that would cause. They would save a small sum in expense, and lose a large amount in the reduction of income, and in the diminished value of real estate.

The interest of a community does not lie in commodities coming a little cheaper to the consumer, but in the production of the greatest quantity of commodities. Wealth does not consist in the cheapness of commodities, but in their quantity, and the greater the quantity produced, the greater will be the wealth of a community.

Low prices, when not caused by the increase of the productive powers of industry, are indicative of low profits, low wages, and of declining wealth in a nation. The gainers by the decline of national wealth from the fall of prices, owing to low profits and low wages, are the fund-holders and the annuitants, and the losers by it are all the rest of the nation.

For notwithstanding they, who live on fixed salaries, are generally inclined to contend, that the interest of the nation consists in the interests of the consumer, and not in that of the producer, yet they would find that the low prices of home products, when not caused by the increase of the productive powers of industry, would have the effect, either to reduce salaries, or to lessen the number of those who lived on them; and that the reduction of the aggregate amount paid in salaries, would be in proportion to the decrease of production resulting from low prices.

IV. ASSUMED EQUALITY OF PROFITS AND WAGES.

Mr. M'Culloch assumes the equality of profits and wages, in the different departments of industry, to be a point incontestably established, and this assumed equality he supposes to be produced by the transfer of capital and labor from those departments, in which profits and wages are low, to the department in which profits and wages are higher. (110.) 'Where-ever industry is free,' he observes, 'the rate of wages earned by the laborers engaged in any particular department of industry, and the rate of profit derived from the capital vested in it, cannot, for any considerable period, either fall below, or rise above, the rate of wages and profits accruing to laborers and capitalists engaged in other departments. (107.) Again he observes, that 'If the rate of wages in one department were depressed below the common level, laborers would leave it to go to others; and if it were to rise above this common level, then it is plain laborers would be attracted from those departments where wages were lower, until the increased supply had sunk them to their just level.' (109.)

Profits and wages, in the different departments of industry, have no common level. Each department has its own, and a different level. The average rate of profits and wages, in the different departments, are permanently different. And this difference is according as there may be more intelligence, skill, ingenuity, and dexterity, employed in one department than another, compared with the quantity of capital they respectively employ.

In the mechanic arts, there is the least capital in proportion to skill employed, and in these arts, consequently, the profits of capital and the wages of labor are higher than in any other department of industry. On the other hand, agriculture employs more capital in proportion to skill, than any other branch of industry; and consequently, the profits of capital and the wages of labor are lower in agriculture, than in any other branch of industry. If profits and wages should rise, in a particular department of industry, above their average rate, they are not brought down to it again, as Mr. M'Culloch supposes, by the transfer of capital and labor to it, from other departments. If wages, for instance, should rise in manufacture, agricultural laborers could not turn to manufacture, to get higher wages, for they have not the skill requisite for that employment; and if wages should fall in manufacture, manufacturing laborers could not resort to field labor, for their habits unfit them for it; neither could carpenters turn to making hats, or bricklayers to making shoes, in order to get more wages.

Wages are not regulated in this way, as Mr. M'Culloch assumes, but by profits. The rise of profits causes a greater demand for labor, and more labor to be employed, which raises the rate of wages. The increased production, which results from this, by reducing profits again, causes the discharge of the additional labor, and wages fall to their average rate; and the additional labor employed in these cases is taken from the unemployed labor belonging to the department which employs it.

And in respect of capital, if the profits on capital in manufacture should be higher in proportion than the profits on capital n agriculture, capital could not be drawn from agriculture to be employed in manufacture. The capital of agriculture is chiefly fixed capital, consisting in land, live stock, buildings, and the implements of husbandry. This capital, it is evident, could not be transferred to manufacture, neither could the fixed capital of manufacture be transferred to agriculture, nor either of them be transferred to commerce, nor to any other branch of business.

If profits in any department of industry should rise above their average rate, additional capital and labor would be employed, until profits again declined to their ordinary level. But the additional employment of capital and labor, in these cases, is so far from diminishing, as Mr. M'Culloch assumes, the employment of capital and labor in other departments of industry, that it actually increases their employment in all. Many millions have recently been added, in this country, to the manufacturing capital, and yet we see, at the same time, both more capital and labor employed in every other kind of business, than there was before. The cause is obvious. The increase of production in manufacture has increased production in every other department of industry. It has, by furnishing the means of a greater demand for the products of the other departments, caused more capital and labor to be employed in production in each, to meet that demand. Therefore, if the additional employment of capital and labor, and the consequent increase of production in one department of industry, actually cause, as they unquestionably do, the additional employment of labor and capital and the consequent increase of production in every other, it is clear that Mr. M'Culloch errs in assuming that the employment of capital and labor is increased in one department only by diminishing it in others. His error upon this point appears to arise from his doctrine, that the capital and labor of a country are always fully employed, and that without a previous increase of capital, no additional labor can be employed. We have already shown this doctrine to be unfounded.

V. REGULATING PRINCIPLE OF VALUE AND PRICE.

Upon the subject of value and price, Mr. M'Culloch observes, that 'The exchangeable value of commodities, when compared with each other, and their value or price when compared with money, is held almost universally to depend on their relative abundance or scarcity in the market, compared with the demand. We believe, however, that we shall be able to show that this opinion rests on no good foundation, and that it is the cost of production, which is the sole regulating principle of price.' (107.) He then, after treating of the equality of wages and profits which he assumes to be established, proceeds upon this assumption, to lay down formally as a principle that 'It is the cost of production, which is the permanent and ultimate regulator of the exchangeable value or price of every commodity, which is not subjected to a monopoly, and which may be indefinitely increased in quantity by the application of fresh capital and labor to its production.' (110.)

This doctrine, which the Editor informs us is one of the leading doctrines of the modern school of Ricardo, we shall endeavor to show is erroneous, and that the common opinions on the subject are correct. And that it is not the cost of production, but the relation between demand and supply, which is the immediate, constant, and permanent regulator of the price of commodities, and that, whether they be subjected to a monopoly or not, or whether they can be indefinitely increased or not.

The existing want, for the products of industry, both for present and future use and consumption, together with the power and will to satisfy it, compared with the present and prospective supply, determines the demand for them. The demand regulates their price, and their price regulates their production. The greater their price, compared with the cost of production, the greater will be the quantity produced, and the less their price, the less will be the quantity produced. Want, with the power to satisfy it, is the cause, and production is the effect, of demand and price.

Mr. M'Culloch's error seems to arise, in part, from his mistaking effect for cause, and considering production to be the cause of price, and consequently, the cost of production to be the regulator of price.

If the cost of production were the regulator of price, an article might be produced in an unlimited quantity, without any reduction of price; but, if individuals were to practice upon this doctrine, they would most assuredly ruin themselves.

Mr. M'Culloch argues, in support of his doctrine, that because it costs more to produce a coach than to produce a hat, a person, however more anxious he may be to have a coach than to have a hat, cannot purchase a coach with the same money that he could purchase a hat; but that, if coaches were to be produced as cheaply as hats, then he might have a coach as cheap as a hat. And to this we might add, that if coaches were as abundant as hats, he might then have a coach as cheap as a hat, even though coaches cost a hundred times as much to produce them; for in such case the demand for coaches would be less than the demand for hats.

'If any great discovery were made in agriculture,' says Mr. M'Culloch, 'such a discovery, for instance, as would reduce the cost of cultivation a half, the price of agricultural produce would fall in the same proportion.' (113.) This is not true. Nothing could reduce the price but a diminution of demand; and nothing could reduce the demand, but either an increase in the quantity of produce, or a diminished consumption. Now as neither of these circumstances is supposed to exist in this case, the diminished cost of production could not diminish the demand, and the price consequently could not fall. The saving here, in the cost of production, instead of reducing the price of produce, would go to increase the rent of land.

Mr. M'Culloch asks, 'why is the price of corn almost invariably higher in this country (Great Britain) than in France? Is it because we have a greater demand for it, or because of the greater cost of production in this country?' (113.) We answer, because there is a greater demand for it in Great Britain, than in France. The demand for it is greater, because the number of individuals, who live by other means than by agriculture, and who consequently require to be supplied with corn, is much greater in Great Britain, in proportion to population, than in France. The increasing demand for an article of which the supply is limited, enhances its price. The introduction of foreign corn being subject to restrictions in Great Britain, the increase of her wealth and population increases the demand for corn of her own growth, and consequently raises its price. The high price of corn, however, when it arises from no other cause than the exclusion of foreign corn, instead of being made a subject of complaint, ought to be considered, as it really is, promotive of the public prosperity. It has the effect to increase the employment of labor in every department of industry. It not only causes the land, which is already in cultivation, to be better cultivated, but it also causes cultivation to be extended to inferior lands, which otherwise would be unproductive and valueless. And thus, by increasing agricultural production, it supplies the means of a greater demand for the products of the other branches of industry, which causes a corresponding increase of production in them, and the more there is produced the greater is the general accumulation of wealth.

Mr. M'Culloch observes that 'a pound weight of gold is at present worth about fifteen pounds of silver;' and that 'the cause of this difference in the price of the two metals consists entirely in the circumstance of its costing about fifteen times as much to produce a pound of gold as to produce a pound of silver.' (113.) Mr. M'Culloch is not correct in stating that it costs fifteen times as much to produce a pound of gold as to produce a pound of silver, unless in the cost he reckons the share which goes to the owner of the mine; and if he does this, even though the gold cost nothing but the labor of raising it pure from the mine, he might say with equal truth, that it cost fifteen times as much as silver. But whether it cost fifteen times more, or fifteen times less than silver to produce it, this circumstance can have no influence on its value; for it is not owing to the greater or less cost of production, but to the greater scarcity of gold than of silver, that the value of gold is so much greater than that of silver. The great value of the diamond is also owing to the same cause, its scarcity, and not to the cost of producing it; for it is not a product of labor, but of nature, and the discovery of chance. If the same quantity of gold, which is annually produced, were to be produced without cost, it would not reduce its value in relation to silver, for while the quantity of one, in relation to the other, remains unaltered, their value in relation to each other would remain the same. If the supply of iron were as limited as that of gold, it would, from its scarcity and superior utility, even though it were found in its pure metallic state and cost nothing to the discoverer but the expense of taking it to market, be in much greater demand than gold, and consequently of more value than gold. This instance alone is sufficient to prove, that it is the want which exists for an article, and not the cost of producing it, that determines its exchangeable value.

Mr. M'Culloch, as a further illustration of his doctrine, takes the instance of cotton goods, and infers, because the price of them is less now than it was sixty years ago, that it is owing to the diminished cost of production. The true explanation of the result in this case, is this, that the diminished cost of production caused a greater quantity to be produced in proportion to the consumption, than what was produced before, and this, reducing the comparative demand, lowered the prices of these goods. The producers, well knowing that demand regulates price, and that the demand, and consequently the price, would be greater in proportion as the supply was less abundant, always endeavored so to proportion their supply to the demand, as that the price resulting from it should repay the cost of production with a profit; hence it is that the price of commodities, in many cases, nearly coincides with the cost of production. But were the cost of production to regulate prices, the price of a commodity would in every instance of bargain and sale correspond exactly with it, whereas we know by experience that it never does, except by chance.

Further, if the cost of production regulated prices, the price of a commodity could not fall below the cost of producing it, were ever so great a quantity to be produced and thrown into the market at once. The price of it, however, in such case, would fall, and the demand, which resulted from the proportion between the supply and the want there might be for the commodity, would determine its price; for it is the comparative abundance, or scarcity of an article, which through demand regulates its price. Cotton goods are much cheaper now than they were sixty years ago, because the production of them is so much greater, in proportion to their consumption, than it was then; and had these goods been, at that distant period, supplied in as great abundance in proportion to the demand, as they are at present, the price of them would have been as low, whatever it might have cost to have produced them.

If a commodity should be produced, for which it might happen there was no demand, it would not sell for any price, whatever the cost of producing it might have been.

And on the other hand, if a commodity, of which the supply cannot be increased, and for which there is a constant demand, were to be produced without cost, its price, from that circumstance, would be none the less. A diminution in the cost of producing a commodity increases the profit on its production, but it has no influence on price otherwise than as the increase of profit, through the competition it raises, causes its production to increase faster than its consumption increases; and it is to its quantity thus accumulating, which reduces the demand for it, that the fall of its price is owing. As the relation between price and the cost of production regulates the quantity produced, so does the relation between demand and the quantity produced regulate prices.

Mr. M'Culloch has, by improperly including profits in the cost of production, confounded the cost of a commodity to the producer, with the cost of it to the consumer; and this has led him, after making an exception of certain commodities which he enumerates, to observe, as well he might, 'that the average price of the various products of art and industry always coincides with the cost of production.' Indeed, without the exception of any commodity whatever, if actual average profits be included in the cost of production, the prices of all commodities must necessarily exactly coincide with the cost of producing them, for the profits make the only difference there ever is between them.

The actual cost of producing commodities, consists in the wages of labor, the interest of the capital employed, and the value of the capital expended in their production. The profits are what prices yield, over and above this cost. Mr. M'Culloch speaks of 'the extreme importance of having correct opinions respecting the regulating principle of price.' (116.) We agree with him that it is important, and would therefore ask him, what practical application could be made of his principle, that would not be mischievous? If the cost of production be the regulator of price, what is there to restrain the producer from any excess of supply? If the cost of production regulates price, how can excess of supply cause prices to fall below it? It is not probable however, that any practical man would ever adopt a theory, so much at variance with his own experience. He is well aware, that demand in relation to supply determines prices, and no theoretical notions would ever induce him to believe to the contrary. He accordingly calculates, so to adjust his supply to the demand, as to secure a price, that will repay him the cost of production, with a profit.

Before we leave this subject, it may be well to notice the different sense in which Mr. M'Culloch often uses, when it suits his purpose, the term demand, from that in which it is commonly used, and from that in which only it can be properly used, when treated of in reference to its influence on price.

Demand is diminished so as to lower prices in two ways, first, by the consumption's diminishing faster than the supply diminishes; secondly, by augmenting the supply faster than the consumption increases. It is in this latter way that the demand for cotton goods in proportion to the supply is reduced, so as to reduce their prices. Yet Mr. M'Culloch says, 'The demand for them has been prodigiously augmented.' (114.) This is true in an absolute sense, but it is not true in its relative sense, compared with the greater supply, in the sense in which he pretended to use it. If he had said the consumption of them, instead of the demand for them, has been prodigiously augmented, his expression would have been correct. The following quotation affords another instance of the misuse of the term demand. 'If the cost of production be diminished, price will be equally diminished, though the demand should be increased to any conceivable extent.' (115.) The price will *not* be diminished, unless the supply be increased, and in that case the demand would be diminished. Mr. M'Culloch erroneously ascribes to cost of production, an effect which is produced solely by excess of supply. Again, he asserts, that 'If the cost of production be increased, price will be equally increased, though the demand should sink to the lowest possible limit.' (115.) This is not true, for whatever a commodity may have cost to produce it, if it be in no demand, it will *not* sell for any price.

VI. MODERN THEORY OF RENT.

We now come to the modern theory of Rent, of which Mr. M'Vickar observes that 'its discovery, or rather its elucidation, is the great glory of the school of Ricardo, and unquestionably the greatest advance which has been made in political economy since the time of Adam Smith.' (129, note.) With all due deference to the opinion of Mr. M'Vickar, as well as to the opinions of other eminent political economists, given in support of the correctness of this theory, we shall proceed to an examination of its principles, and endeavour to ascertain upon what sort of foundation it rests.

As Mr. Ricardo states the theory with more precision and perspicuity than Mr. M'Culloch, and lets us perceive more clearly in what it differs from the commonly received opinions, we shall first give his general view of it. 'On the first settling of a country,' says Mr. Ricardo, 'in which there is an abundance of rich and fertile land, a very small proportion of which is required to be cultivated for the support of the actual population, there will be no rent.'—'When, in the progress of society, land of the second degree of fertility is taken into cultivation, rent immediately commences on that of the first quality, and the amount of that rent will depend on the difference in the quality of these two portions of land.'—'When land of the third quality is taken into cultivation, rent immediately commences on the second, and it is regulated as before, by the difference in their productive powers. At the same time, the rent of the first quality will rise, for that must always be above the rent of the second, by the difference between the produce which they yield, with a given quantity of capital and labor. With every step in the progress of population, which shall oblige a country to have recourse to land of a worse quality, to enable it to raise its supply of food, rent on all the more fertile land will rise.'—'It is only then because land is of different qualities, with respect to its productive powers, and because, in the progress of population, land of an inferior quality, or less advantageously situated, is called into cultivation, that rent is ever paid for the use of it.'

According to this theory then, no rent would ever be paid, in the progress of population, if all lands were of equal quality, and equally advantageously situated! This principle cannot be admitted. It is *not* because land is of *different qualities*, that it yields rent, but first, because, it is limited in quantity and individually appropriated; secondly, because it will support with its produce more persons than what are required for its cultivation; and thirdly, because, with the progress of population, there are more persons than what are required for its cultivation, to be supported by its produce. One person pays rent for another person's land, not because one piece of land is better than another, but because he can make a profit by the cultivation of it, besides paying the rent. If all lands were of *equal quality*, and there were more persons to be supported by the produce of them than what owned them, they would all pay rent, not equal rents however, unless they were all equally well situated with respect to markets. Inferior land, in the vicinity of a large market-town, would pay a greater rent than superior land at a distance from it. It is *not* therefore, because some land is superior to other land, that a rent is paid for the use of land. We cannot command the use of another's property for our benefit, without paying an equivalent for the advantage we receive from it. We pay a rent for the use of land as we pay a rent for the use of a house, or pay interest for the use of money;—we pay, because the owners of these different kinds of capital will not part with the use of them without being paid for it, and because we derive an advantage from their use, equivalent to the rent or interest we pay. Thus, it appears, it is not from the difference in quality, but from the exclusive possession of land, and because many want the use of what few exclusively possess, that rent arises. It is with capital in land, as with capital in houses, or capital in money, or in any other description of property. A rent or interest is paid to the owners, for their use, in proportion to the demand there may respectively be for them. Were all the lands of Great Britain of equal quality, and equally advantageously situated, they would yield equal rents; and were the lands of such quality, as that the aggregate quantity of produce, raised from them, were to be the same as at present, the sum-total of rents would likewise be the same; for it is not, as Mr. Ricardo supposes, the cost of production on the worst soils cultivated, which regulates the price of produce, but it is the quantity of produce raised, compared with the demand for it, which determines the price, and it is the *price of the produce which regulates the rent.*

We will now endeavor to account for the rise and progress of rent in a less artificial manner, than that which Mr. Ricardo has adopted. On the first settlement of a country, the lands most advantageously situated, as well as those most fertile, are immediatly taken up, and individually appropriated. At this time when population is thin and scattered, and when every man is a farmer, and there is none to buy his produce, it is obvious, that lands can produce no rent. But as population increases cultivation is extended, and all the land is at length appropriated.

While population is thus advancing, other employments gradually arise beside that of farming. As this takes place, markets form for agricultural produce, and rent now commences on those lands, which are best situated in respect of the markets. With the progress of wealth and population, the demand for agricultural produce increases, and in proportion as the demand for it increases faster than the supply, the price of it rises, and it is the rise of the price of produce, which causes the rise of rents.

Having arrived thus far, in tracing the progress of rent, and shown that the rise of rent, is owing *to the rise of produce*, caused by the increase of demand resulting from the increase of wealth and population, we would now request particular attention to two separate effects proceeding from *this rise in the price of produce*, which are entirely unconnected with each other. The first is, the gradual extension of cultivation to lands of inferior quality. And the other is, the gradual rise of rent on all the land already cultivated. For it is from Mr. Ricardo having mistaken these two unconnected, though coincident, effects of the same cause, to be cause and effect, one to the other, that his erroneous theory of rent has arisen.

We next proceed to the application, which Mr. Ricardo makes of his theory. 'When land,' he observes, 'of an inferior quality is taken into cultivation, the exchangeable value of raw produce will rise, because more labor is required to produce it.' This is not true. It is not because inferior land is taken into cultivation, that the price of produce rises. The reverse of it is true. It is because the price of produce has already risen, by the increase of demand, that the inferior land is taken into cultivation, and it is the previous rise in price, which pays for the additional labor employed on the inferior soil, to raise the same quantity of produce. The taking the inferior land into cultivation is so far, indeed, from being a cause of the rise of the price of produce, that it has directly the opposite effect. It increases the supply of produce, and thereby operates to reduce its price. This error of Mr. Ricardo, it will be perceived, arises from his mistaking effect for cause. It is the previous rise in the price of produce, which causes the inferior land to be cultivated, and not the cultivation of this, which causes the rise in the price of produce.

'That corn,' says Mr. Ricardo, which is producedwith the greatest quantity of labor, is the regulator of the price of corn, and rent does not and cannot enter in the least degree as a component part of the price.' (48.) The price of corn neither depends on the quantity of labor employed to produce it, nor on the rent of land upon which it is produced. The price of it is solely regulated by the quantity produced, compared

ments were made in agriculture, or in the art of raising corn, as would enable the supply to be obtained from land of the first quality, the price would necessarily and infallibly fall to the precise sum that paid the expenses of its cultivators, and rent would entirely disappear.'(126.) In respect of the first, we have already shown, that the price could not fall unless the supply were increased in relation to demand. In regard to the second, that rent would entirely disappear, its absurdity is obvious. The lands in Europe are owned by less than a tenth of its inhabitants. Now if the owners of this land 'of the first quality' would not permit it to be cultivated, beyond what was necessary for their own supply, without being paid rent, as most assuredly they would not, it is very clear that the other nine tenths of the inhabitants could not get their supply of corn without paying the rent.

The following quotation is the last we shall present on this subject. 'As the rent is nothing but the excess, or the value of the excess, of the produce obtained from the best above that obtained from the very worst soils in cultivation, it is plain it does not enter into the cost of production.'(148.) If 'rent be nothing but the excess, or the value of the excess, of the produce obtained from the best above that obtained from the worst soils in cultivation,' how happens it, that lands in the vicinity of large market-towns pay rent, while other lands at a certain distance, of superior fertility, and which yield greater quantities of produce, pay no rent? Rent does not, we repeat, arise from the superiority of one soil to another, but it arises rom the profits of cultivation, and these profits are not regulated y the differences in soils, but by the prices of produce in the istrict where it is raised.

With respect to Mr. M'Culloch's position, that rent does not ter into the cost of production, it may be observed, that it is consistent with his doctrine, that the cost of production coines with average prices. For it is very plain that the prices produce repay, not only the cost of the labor and capital

with the demand. It is not the cost of the corn, which is produced with the greatest quantity of labor, that regulates the price of corn, but it is, on the contrary, the price of corn, which determines how great a quantity of labor may be employed to produce it. The farmer does not practice on Mr. Ricardo's theory, that the portion of corn, which is raised at the greatest expense, fixes the price of the whole crop, but he calculates, from the actual price, how much he may venture to expend in cultivation, so as to be sure, if the price hold good, of a remuneration, that will replace to him the expenses with a profit.

To return again to Mr. M'Culloch,—he lays it down as a principle, that 'Rent increases, when the profits of agricultural labor diminish, and diminishes, when they increase;' and as an inference from it, that 'Profits are at their maximum in countries like Indiana and Illinois, and generally in all situations, in which no rent is paid.' (121.) Now both the principle, and the inference, are at variance with the facts in the case. Rent does not increase, as agricultural profits diminish, but on the contrary, rent increases as agricultural profits increase. They are both effects of the same cause, a rise in the price of agricultural produce, by the increase of demand, which, by raising agricultural profits above their average-rate, raises the rent in the same proportion. The rent rises just so far as to absorb this excess of profit, and the agricultural profits remain, as they were before, undiminished. The inference from this erroneous principle, that profits are at their maximum in countries like Indiana and Illinois, is equally opposed to the truth in the case. In Indiana and Illinois, there are no profits on the employment of capital and labor in cultivation. The farmer, by his own labor, raises produce enough for the support of his family; but, owing to the great distance of markets, and the little demand there is for produce at home, were he to employ hired labor and capital in cultivation, the price of the produce would not replace to him half the cost of raising it.

'A rent is paid,' says Mr. M'Culloch, 'because the demand is such, that it cannot be supplied without cultivating soils of a diminished decree of fertility, as compared with the best.'(121.) A rent is not paid from that cause. The same amount of rent would be paid, if the same demand were to be supplied with the same quantity of produce, from soils, all of equal fertility. The cause of rent, as we have already stated, is such a demand for produce, as raises the price of it above the cost of the labor and capital expended in production. A rent is paid, because the price of produce is so high, as to yield to the cultivator a sum, which exceeds the cost of production, including the average-profits. This excess the cultivator pays over to the landlord, for the use of the land as rent. Different degrees of fertility in soils merely determine the difference of rents, not the amount of rents. It is the demand for produce compared with the quantity supplied, without any regard to whether it be grown on soils of different degrees of fertility, or all on a soil of equal fertility, which determines the price of it, and it is this price which determines the amount of rents.

Mr. M'Culloch observes, 'that although landlords were to give up the whole of their rents, their doing so would have no influence on the price of corn.' (122.) This is true; and he might have added with equal truth, that were the laborers on the same land to give up the whole of their wages, their doing so would have no more influence on the price of corn than the landlords relinquishing their rents. Both cases are governed by the same principle, that is, that the supply of corn, compared with the demand, would not be increased by the relinquishment of rent and wages. And the relinquishment of wages could have no more effect to increase the supply, than the relinquishment of rent. Both, however, would diminish the cost of production to the cultivator. But, as the price of corn depends on the quantity raised, compared with the demand, and not on the cost of production, and as the relinquishment of wages and rents, would not increase the supply from lands

which pay rents, the price of corn would not from that cir
cumstance be reduced. The cost of production has no infl
ence on price, except as it tends to augment or diminish t
supply in relation to demand. Therefore, however much
cost of producing a commodity might be reduced, unless
supply were increased in consequence of it, the reductic
cost would have no influence on its price.

'It is,' Mr. M'Culloch observes, 'by the cost of prod
that portion of the required supply of corn which is pr
in the most unfavorable circumstances, and with the
expense, that the average price of all the rest must
be regulated.' (121.) This is an erroneous position.
already shown that the price of corn is regulated sole
quantity produced compared with the demand.
however, that the cost of that portion of corn, wh
ed on the worst soils, or at the greatest expense,
nearly coincides with the average price of all
because that portion regulates the price of the w
cause the price of corn enables the cultivator
how much he can safely expend in raising that
price of corn is the cause, and not the eff
portions being raised. Mr. M'Culloch's error
his mistaking what was the effect of price fo

It is the price of produce, which, by enab
to calculate how much he may venture to e
cultivation to inferior soils with a prospe
causes the coincidence, which Mr. M'C
neously as cause and effect in the foll
no case, whether the demand be great
of raw produce ever permanently ex
sum necessary to pay the cost of pr
the supply, that is raised on the wor
capital laid out on the soil.' (122.)

Here follow two very extravagant
ever extent the demand might incr

expended in cultivation, but they repay to the cultivator besides, the whole amount he pays to the landlord in rent. Therefore if rent does not enter into the cost of production, there is no such coincidence between the average cost of production, and the average prices of products, as according to his doctrine there ought to be. But when a theory is founded on erroneous principles, it is not easy to make its different parts harmonize.

To exemplify this yet further. If we suppose rent to enter into the cost of production, as it really does, it would conflict no less with another doctrine, which Mr. M'Culloch maintains, which is, that nothing enters into the cost of producing commodities but the 'immediate labor, and the accumulated labor or capital, which have been necessarily laid out in their production' (130); and capital he defines to be nothing more than the accumulated produce of anterior labor. (129.)

The rent of land is only another term for the interest of capital; and the interest of capital, employed in production, is considered as much an item, as the wages of labor, in making up the cost of the products. The tenant hires capital in land, as the trader hires capital in money, or as the manufacturer hires capital in machinery, or as the mechanic hires capital in work-shops and tools,—they all hire it because they can make more by the employment of it than they pay the owners for the use of it. And what they pay for the use of it, whether it be called interest or rent, for it is the same thing, is a charge, which enters into the cost of the commodities they respectively produce for sale; and the prices they get for them cover their cost, besides leaving to the producers their average profits..

VII. EXCHANGEABLE VALUE.

The exchangeable value of commodities is regulated, says Mr. M'Culloch, 'by the total quantity of immediate labor, and of accumulated labor, or capital, which have been necessarily laid out in their production.' (130.) This principle is not correct. It is at variance with uniform experience. Experience teaches, that it is the greater or less quantity of one commodity than of another in the market, compared with the demand for each, which regulates respectively their relative value. If the quantity of any one commodity remain stationary, while that of all others be augmented, the value of that commodity will be augmented proportionately. A larger quantity of every other must be given in exchange for that.

Again, if the supply of every commodity, except corn, should be increased in equal proportions, and the supply of that remain unaltered, the value of each in relation to corn would be diminished, while in relation to each other their value would remain the same. In this case more of every commodity must be given in exchange for corn.

Further, if the quantity of money should be increased, while that of every other commodity remained stationary, the value of money in relation to other commodities would be reduced, while the value of all other commodities in relation to each other would remain unchanged. In other words, the price of all commodities would be enhanced; by price meaning the money price, for we know no other kind of price. Now, if it be true that these variations in exchangeable value are regulated by variations in relative quantities, or in other words, by variations in the proportion between supply and demand, which no one of any experience can doubt, Mr. M'Culloch's position, that the exchangeable value of commodities is regulated by the total quantity of labor, immediate and anterior, expended in their production, must necessarily be erroneous. 'Capital' Mr. M'Culloch here defines to be 'nothing more than the accumulated produce of anterior labor.' (129.) This definition is not sufficiently comprehensive. It excludes all that portion of capital, which is a gift of nature, and not the result of labor, such as capital in land, in mines, in quarries, and so forth; and these all, when individually appropriated, are capital in the hands of those who possess them. They are employed for purposes of income or profit, and have an exchangeable value in proportion to the income they yield or the profit they afford. Mr. Ricardo has given a definition, which is more nearly correct. 'Capital,' he says, 'is that part of the wealth of a country, which is employed in production.' As this however does not seem to include the capital employed in trade, in transportation, in wharves, warehouses, bridges, turnpikes, canals, and so forth, we think the more correct definition to be, that capital is that portion of wealth, which is employed for purposes of income or profit. We have noticed Mr. M'Culloch's incorrect definition of capital, in order to show that 'the principle, which makes the exchangeable value of commodities dependant on the quantities of labor required for their production,' (130) is not only erroneous in the connexion in which we have already considered it, but also in relation to the value of the capital, which enters into the cost of producing commodities.

Mr. M'Culloch confines his view of the value of the capital, which enters into their production, to that value alone which is the result of anterior labor, whereas it is plain that other values in capital, beside that, enter into the cost of producing them,—values, which arise from the exclusive possession of land, for instance, the value of the timber-tree as it stands in the forest, stone as it lies in the quarry, minerals as they are found in the mines, in short, the value of all rude materials in their natural state, which enter into the production of commodities.

Having already shown that the exchangeable value of commodities is not regulated by the cost of their production, it is hardly necessary to observe, that their exchangeable value cannot be dependant on that portion of the cost of producing them, which is exclusive of the cost of the rude materials, which enter into their production.

VIII. EXCHANGEABLE VALUE IN RELATION TO WAGES.

'It now only remains,' observes Mr. M'Culloch, 'to trace the effects of fluctuations in the rate of wages on price.' (132.) Mr. M'Culloch's conclusions on this subject are governed by principles, which we have already shown to be erroneous; and although his conclusions may be strictly drawn from the premises which he assumes, yet as these premises are erroneous, the deduction from them must be so also. There is however an error of a different nature, which pervades his reasoning on this subject, and that is, his considering the fluctuations in the rate of wages, as arising from an independent principle of action, inherent in the nature of wages, and not as the effect of a general cause, which, while it regulates variations in exchangeable value, regulates at the same time fluctuations in profits and wages.

Variations in the rate of wages are the effect of those variations in the demand for labor, which proceed from a rise or fall of the prices of the products of labor. And the rise or fall of the prices of the products of labor, is caused by the supply of these products falling short of, or exceeding, the demand there may be for them. But Mr. M'Culloch, in treating of fluctuations in the rate of wages, as exercising an independent and controlling influence over exchangeable value, rejects entirely from consideration the principle, which actually regulates exchangeable value, namely, the demand for commodities in relation to their supply, and which principle, also, by regulating exchangeable value, regulates the rise and fall of profits and wages.

Mr. M'Culloch states, that 'When every class of producers employ either fixed or circulating capitals of precisely the same degree of durability, they must be all equally affected by a rise or fall of wages. This is a principle, which is equally assented to by Mr. Ricardo and Mr. Malthus, and which is indeed self-evident. But when such is the case, it is plainly impossible that a rise or fall of wages can occasion any variation in the exchangeable or comparative value of commodities.' (132.) We shall show to the contrary.

A rise of wages never takes place without some cause. This cause is an increased demand for the products of any one or more of the different branches of industry, which has the effect gradually to increase the demand for the products of all.

We will now suppose this increased demand to have taken place, for the products of agriculture. The consequence of it would be, by raising the price of produce, to augment the profits of cultivation. This would increase the demand for labor, and the increased demand for labor would raise the wages of labor. Cultivation would be extended to inferior soils, and as much additional labor would be employed, as the rise in the price of produce would admit of being employed with the ordinary rate of profit. But, as the rise of wages would increase the demand for produce, nearly or quite as much as the additional labor would increase the supply, the rise in the price of produce would still be maintained.

Now, on the other hand, let us see what would be the result in manufacture. And that the circumstances in the two cases may correspond with the circumstances, under which Mr. M'Culloch has stated his principle, we will suppose, first, that the same quantity of labor is employed by manufacture as by agriculture, and that the labor in both produces equal amounts of exchangeable value, beside keeping their fixed and circulating capitals equally good, which is the same thing as though the capitals of both were of equal durability; and then we will suppose an increased demand to have taken place for the products of manufacture. The consequence of it would be, a rise in the price of manufactured goods. This would increase competition among manufacturers, which would increase the demand for labor. The increased demand for labor would raise the wages of the laborer. More workmen would be employed. The manufacturing machinery would be increased, and a greater quantity of goods would be produced. Thus would the supply progressively augment, until the prices went down again, to a point, at which they would just return a remunerating profit to the manufacturer.

At this point the supply would be so adjusted to the demand, that prices would vary very little from it. Competition would prevent their rising much above, and the interest of the manufacture would prevent their going much below.

Thus we see, contrary to Mr. M'Culloch's doctrine, and under the same circumstances, that a rise in the rate of wages is followed by a very different result in manufacture, from what it is in agriculture. Not, however, that the result in either case is owing, as Mr. M'Culloch supposes, to a rise of wages; for it is very clear that the rise of wages, and the results in both cases, are different effects of one and the same cause, namely, the demand for their respective products, compared with the supply.

The increased demand for agricultural produce augmented its exchangeable value. Its value did not decline again, because the supply could not be augmented, compared with the demand. Whereas, although the increased demand for the products of manufacture, at first augmented their exchangeable value, yet competition, by augmenting the supply as compared with the demand, soon reduced it again to about its former standard.

We thus prove, that the positions which we have quoted are erroneous, by showing that variations in relative values do *not* depend on variations in the rate of wages, and that the values of products of different branches of industry are actually changed in relation to each other, in those cases, in which Mr. M'Culloch contends they would remain unaltered.

Mr. Ricardo not only showed,' says Mr. M'Culloch, 'that it was impossible for any rise of wages to raise the price of all commodities, but he also showed that in many cases a rise of wages necessarily led to a fall of prices, and a fall of wages to a rise of prices.' (134.)

Mr. Ricardo's erroneous conclusions here result, first, from his mistaking effect for cause, and secondly, from his considering 'the immediate and interior labor,' fixed in commodities, to be the sole regulator of their relative values.

The rise in the price of commodities *always precedes* the rise in the rate of wages, and it is this rise in the price of commodities, which, by increasing the demand for labor, is the *cause* of the rise of wages. And it is the natural tendency of the rise of commodities in price, by causing additional labor to be employed, to augment their supply compared with the demand, and thus again to reduce their price, together with the wages, of labor, to about their former level.

Mr. M'Culloch attempts to demonstrate the position, 'that, in many cases, a rise of wages necessarily led to a fall of prices,' in the following manner. 'Suppose,' says he, 'a manufacturer has a machine worth £20,000, of a high degree of durability, and which can without the assistance of any manual labor produce commodities. If profits were at ten per cent. the commodities produced by this machine, would sell for £2000, together with a small addition to replace its wear and tear. Now it is quite certain, that if, from any cause whatever, profits rise or fall, the price of the goods, produced by this machine, would also rise or fall. If profits were to rise to 15 per cent. the price of the goods produced by the machine must, in order that its owner may obtain the same profit with other capitalists, rise to £3000, and if, on the other hand, profits fall to five per cent. the price of his goods must, for the same reason, fall to £1000. If, therefore, it can be shown, that a rise of wages reduces the rate of profits, it is plain it must also reduce the exchangeable value, or price, of all such commodities as are chiefly produced by machinery.' (135.)

He then, after endeavoring to prove that the rise of wages has this effect, comes to the conclusion that 'it is absolutely certain, that profits fall when wages rise, and rise when wages fall; and thus, he seems to think, he has demonstrated the proposition, that a rise of wages in many cases, causes a fall of prices.

He has, however, totally failed; for it is self-evident, that the price of the goods made by the machine, must be governed by the average price of the same kind of goods made without the machine; and consequently, that a rise in the wages of labor, could not reduce the price of the goods made by the machine without the aid of labor, unless it reduced the price of the same kind of goods made without the machine by manual labor; and this it is impossible that a rise of wages should ever do.

Besides, had Mr. M'Culloch been able to show, that a rise of wages reduces profits, which he is not, it would not have proved any thing to his purpose in this case; for as the machine is supposed to produce commodities without manual labor, it is clear that the value of the commodities, or, in other words, the profits of the machine, are not subject to the supported control of average profits. On the contrary, the amount of the profit of the machine would be just equal to the amount of the profit of the capital, and the wages of the labor together, enployed in the common way, in producing a like quantity of the same kind of goods. Or what is the same thing, the value of the commodities produced by the machine, would be equal to the value of a like quantity of the same kind of goods, produced by labor and capital in the usual manner. Mr. Ricardo has endeavored to demonstrate the position, by fallacious argument similar to that of Mr. M'Culloch.

In no case whatever, does a rise of wages cause a fall of prices, or a fall of wages cause a rise of prices. On the contrary, it is the previous rise of the prices alone, which leads to a rise of wages, and the previous fall of prices to a fall of wages. The rise or fall of wages is the effect, and not the cause, of a rise or fall of prices. And whatever the proportion may be, between the fixed and circulating capital, or between the greater or less durability of the capitals employed in conjunction with labor, in the production of commodities, the rise and fall of their prices will be altogether independent of the rise and fall of wages. It is the greater or less quantity of labor, and not the greater or less wages paid the laborers, that augments or diminishes the supply of commodities in relation to their demand, and it is this alone, which determines the rise and fall of their prices.

IX. PROFITS IN RELATION TO WAGES.

Mr. M'Culloch treats of the relation of profits to wages, in the same inverted and unnatural order, in which we have seen he treats of the connexion between exchangeable value, and wages; and the fallacy of his reasoning on this subject arises in part from the same source,—mistaking effect for cause. He erroneously assumes that profits are controlled by wages; whereas, on the contrary, it is the rate of profits which controls the rate of wages. 'It is absolutely certain,' he asserts, 'that profits vary inversely as wages, that is, they fall when wages rise, and rise when wages fall.' (136.) We shall soon show these propositions to be unfounded.

The rise of profits, in all cases, always precedes, and is the cause of the rise of wages, and the fall of profits in like manner is the cause of the fall of wages. The increase of demand for the products of industry enhances their prices. This *raises* the *profits* on their production. The *increase of profits* increases the demand for labor, and *this raises the wages of the laborer.* Now, unless the owner of capital could augment his profits by employing additional labor, he would not employ it, and if he did not, the wages of labor could not rise. But if he does employ additional labor, notwithstanding the rise of wages it causes, it affords complete evidence that he augments his profits by so doing; from which it must necessarily follow, that a rise of wages cannot cause a fall of profits. Further, a rise in the price of agricultural produce, by increasing the profits of cultivation, increases the demand for labor, and raises wages. Now if at these high wages the farmer employs additional labor, and extends cultivation to inferior soils, it is because he can augment the amount of his profit by so doing; and though the rate of profits may in this case be diminished, yet the aggregate amount of his profits will be enlarged.

'The fall of profits,' observes Mr. M'Culloch, 'which invariably takes place as society advances and population becomes denser, is not owing to competition, but to a different cause,—to a diminution of the power to employ capital with advantage, resulting either from a decrease in the fertility of the soil, which must be taken into cultivation in the progress of society, or from an increase of taxation.' (145.)

This conclusion is incorrect. The same fall in the rate of profits would take place, all other circumstances the same, although the soil were all of an equal degree of fertility. The fall in the rate of profits, which takes place with the increase of wealth and population, is owing to the capital, employed in the different departments of industry, increasing faster than the means increase to employ it with the same advantage. The farmer's capital in land rises in value with the rise in the price of produce. As produce rises, he extends cultivation to inferior soils, and though from this circumstance the *rate* of his profits on the value of his capital be less, yet the *amount* of his profits in the aggregate will be greater.

The merchant finds, that with the increase of capital and competition in commerce, the rate of profit is diminished, but that the sum total of profit is augmented. The manufacturer and mechanic experience the same thing, that the increase of capital increases competition among them, and lowers the *rate* of profits, while the *aggregate amount* of profit is increasing. Mr. M'Culloch contends that 'Rent does not enter into price. Wages and profits make up the whole value of every commodity.' (148.) We would ask him, what there is, besides rent, which enters into the value, or price, of trees as they stand in the forest, of building stone as it lies in the quarry, and of ores as they lie in the mines?

Mr. M'Culloch, in support of his doctrine on wages and profits, quotes the following passage from Mr. Ricardo. 'High wages equally affect the profits of the farmer, the manufacturer, and the merchant. There is no other way of keeping profits up, but by keeping wages down.'(149.) A doctrine which leads to such a conclusion as this,—a conclusion at once totally devoid of truth, and directly opposed to liberal sentiment, to the public interest, and to the well-being of nine tenths of a nation, to the well-being of all those who live by labor,—cannot be too strongly reprobated. We have already proved this doctrine to be altogether erroneous, but it may not be amiss, in further evidence of it, to refer to the results of our own experience. The rate of profits in every department of industry in this country, except in that of farming, is higher, than it is in any other country; and yet the American merchant, manufacturer, and mechanic, pay higher real wages for the labor they employ, than is paid in the same employments in any other nation. High wages are the result of high profits, and the evidence of increasing wealth. Low wages, on the contrary, as for example in some of the northern nations of Europe, are the result of low profits, and the evidence of stationary or declining wealth.

The following quotations afford an exemplification of the 'superior acuteness' of the modern school, in the art of establishing conclusions. Mr. M'Culloch, instead of ascertaining what the facts are in a case, and drawing his inferences from them, finds what they ought to be by his theory, and without hesitation states them to be facts. Thus he asserts 'that profits are at their maximum in countries like Indiana and Illinois.'(121.) And again, that 'the American laborer receives a less proportion of the produce raised by him than the British laborer, and profits are consequently high in America.' (150.) Now there is not the least truth in either of these assertions. The American laborer, in the first place, receives much higher money wages than the British laborer; and, in the second place, he gets for his money a much greater quantity of produce than the British laborer can for the same money.

In fact, the American laborers receive a proportion of the produce raised by them so much greater than the British laborer, that if American laborers, hired at the average rate of wages, were to raise all the produce, which is raised in Indiana and Illinois,—the two States in which, according to Mr. M'Culloch's theory, profits ought to be at their maximum,—the whole produce raised by them would not sell for enough to pay them their wages. And thus it is with the general conclusions of this theory; they are directly contradicted by the actual results of experience.

X. CONSUMPTION.

Mr. M'Culloch observes that 'consumption, in the sense in which the word is used by political economists, is synonymous with use.' (155.) If some economists use it in this sense, they use it improperly. The words have very different meanings. As for example. Flour is used in bread and consumed in food. Wool is used in cloth and consumed in clothing. A house is not said to be consumed, because it is used. We use money in the exchange of commodities, but this is not the consumption of money. A diamond is used for ornament, but it is not said to be consumed for ornament.

To confound the use of words so different in sense, leads to a confusion of ideas; and there is no necessity for it, unless the object be to render the enquiry more obscure, that it may appear to be more profound. Consumption Mr. M'Culloch divides into productive and unproductive consumption. All consumption is unproductive. A hat is no more productive when worn by a laborer, than it is when worn by a man who is not a laborer; consumption is the reverse of production. All men are the consumers of wealth, but all men are not the producers of wealth.

XI. PRODUCTIVE LABOR.

We now come to the question,—What is productive labor? —Adam Smith denominates those, who are engaged in the production of wealth, 'productive laborers,' and those who are not engaged in the production of wealth, 'unproductive laborers,' and in considering this subject, he admits of no other kind of wealth than material wealth.

Mr. M'Culloch, on the contrary, contends that, on this point, 'the whole of Dr. Smith's reasoning proceeds on a false hypothesis,' and that 'he has made a distinction where there is none, and where there can be none.' (164.) The distinction which Dr. Smith makes is consistent with what he considers to be the nature of wealth; and as he admits of no other kind of wealth, than *material* wealth, it follows of course, that he cannot consider any other kind of labor to be productive labor, than that, which is employed in the production of material wealth. We cannot say so much for the consistency of Mr. M'Culloch's doctrine, in this respect, with his general theory on the nature of wealth.

Those, who agree with Dr. Smith, hold that all the labors, which are successively expended on a commodity to add to its exchangeable value, before it gets into the hands of the consumer, are productive labors, and that all the labor, which may be expended on it afterwards, as it has no such object and adds nothing to exchangeable value, is not productive labor.

Mr. M'Culloch contends that there is no difference whatever between the labor of a manufacturer and the labor of the menial servant. 'They are,' he says, 'either both productive, or both unproductive.' (163.) 'The manufacturer,' he observes, 'is not a producer of matter, but of *utility only*, and is it not obvious that the labor of the menial servant is also productive of utility? If for example, the labor expended in converting the wool of the sheep into a coat be, as it unquestionably is, productive, then surely the labor expended in cleaning and brushing the coat, and rendering it fit to be worn, must be so too.' (163.) The fallacy of this argument is very evident. Mr. M'Culloch assumes what is not true, namely, that the manufacturer is a producer of *utility only*. The manufacturer, besides adding utility to the raw material, adds to it exchangeable value also; but the menial servant, by brushing a coat, does not add to its exchangeable value, he only adds to its utility. If to brush a coat added to its exchangeable value, it would be adding to the exchangeable value of an orange to pare it to eat.

'The amusements furnished by players, singers, and so forth,' Mr. M'Culloch observes, 'create new wants, and by so doing stimulate our industry to produce the means of gratifying them; they are really therefore a means of production.' (155.) If players, singers, and so forth, are to be considered productive laborers, because the amusement they afford creates new wants, then the highwayman, who takes our purse, may be considered as a productive laborer, for he also creates a new want.

Productive labor is the labor employed in the production of wealth. Therefore, if the music of the fiddler and the buffoonery of the harlequin be wealth, then the producers of these things are productive laborers, but not otherwise. If these productions be wealth, it is not that kind of wealth, of which political economy treats. This treats only of substantial wealth, such as the fiddler and the buffoon get in exchange for their unsubstantial production.

Mr. M'Culloch further observes, 'that the productiveness of the higher class of public functionaries, mentioned by Dr. Smith, is still more obvious (than that of singers and players.) So far indeed from being unproductive, they are, when they discharge properly the duties of their high station, the most productive laborers in a state.'(165.) No one doubts the utility of their labors, but their's is mental labor. It is not directed to the production of wealth. It merely directs, in providing for the security and defence of the commonwealth, a portion of the wealth produced by physical labor to that object. Another portion of the same wealth, they take to themselves as a compensation for their mental labors in the public service.

When intellectual labor, consisting in the exercise of intelligence, skill and invention, superintends and directs manual labor, and augments its power of producing material wealth, it is then called productive labor. But when only employed in intellectual production, it is, in reference to material wealth, denominated unproductive labor; and as to its relation to intellectual wealth, that does not come within the investigation of political economy. The determination of this question, however, as to what is productive labor and what is not, is of no manner of importance, except as, in admitting the distinction of Dr. Smith, we prescribe bounds to the enquiries of political economy, and limit them to what relates to material wealth. But Mr. M'Culloch, to be consistent with his doctrine on this question, ought to extend his investigations throughout every department of human knowledge. He should point out the means of increasing mental production in all its variety of forms. He should analyze the products, show the value of their component parts, and the manner in which their value is distributed. And as he contends that the labors of public functionaries, of lawyers, physicians, and clergymen,—of menial servants,—of players, singers, dancers, buffoons, and so forth,—are all productive labors, he should show how this kind of productive labor might be increased, and how its powers of production might be augmented; for it is by increasing the quantity and augmenting the power of productive labor, that the progress of national wealth is accelerated.

It is hardly necessary to observe, that Mr. M'Culloch's doctrine on this point is altogether inconsistent with his general doctrines, in relation to the production and distribution of wealth, and also inconsistent with his definition of political economy, which includes his definition of wealth, described by him as altogether material.

XII. VENT FOR COMMODITIES.

Mr. M'Culloch on this subject observes, that 'the true and only encouragement to industry consists in the increase of production.' (167.) This is not correct. If the increase of production be the only encouragement to industry, and production should not actually be on the increase, it would be absolutely impossible, in such case, that any encouragement should ever be given to industry. The increase of industry must always precede the increase of production. The cause must precede its effect. Nothing can be an encouragement to industry, which does not increase its profits; and where the industry of a country is chiefly agricultural, and its supply of produce already exceeds the demand for it, both at home and abroad, it is clear that any increase of production would diminish profits, and instead of encouraging, discourage industry. The only way to encourage industry in the existing branches, is to encourage to the establishment of new branches. The increase of production in these, will then encourage to the increase of industry in the former, and in this way only does the increase of production encourage industry. Mr. M'Culloch seemed to have some vague notion of the truth; but he departed very far from it, in laying down the above proposition.

Again he says, that 'every new product necessarily forms a new equivalent, or a new means of purchasing some other product.' (267.) This is not true as a general principle; it is true only in a limited sense. It is true only when the new product is in demand. If it be not in demand, it will not furnish the means of purchasing any other product. For example, when the supply of corn is already in excess, to double the quantity, by a new supply, would diminish its exchangeable value more than half. The double supply, therefore, would not now purchase so great a quantity of other products, as the single supply would previously purchase.

'It must always be remembered,' says Mr. M'Culloch, 'that the mere existence of a demand, how intense soever it may be, cannot of itself be a means of encouraging production. To become a real demander, a man must not only have the will, but he must also have the power, to purchase the commodity he wishes to possess.' (168.) When we speak of *a demand* for a commodity, we always understand a demand, which includes both the power and will to purchase it. The want of a commodity, without the power and will to purchase it, is never called *the demand* for a commodity. We never consider the wants of the mendicant to constitute a demand for commodities.

XIII. INDIVIDUAL EXPENDITURE.

In respect of individual expenditure, or personal expense, Mr. M'Culloch has adopted the erroneous doctrine of Smith, that it has the effect to diminish productive industry. This doctrine rests on the assumed premises, that the profusion of the rich diminishes capital; that capital cannot be increased, unless through the savings of parsimony; and that without a previous increase of capital no additional labor can be employed. (161.) As we have already shown these propositions to be entirely unfounded, we shall confine our remarks on this doctrine to other points.

In the first place, it may be observed, that this doctrine makes no distinction between the savings of individuals who belong to the unproductive classes in society, and the savings of those who belong to the productive classes; whereas there is the greatest difference between the effects of the two. In the former case, the savings, if not at first, yet ultimately, go to increase the employment of unproductive labor in personal service. In the latter case, the savings are used to increase the employment of productive labor, in the production of wealth.

Besides, profusion can never proceed from the pursuits and habits of the productive classes ; their great object is accumulation ; this is their ruling passion, and industry and economy their governing principles. Profusion is witnessed only among the rich of the unproductive classes ; and as their savings would finally go to increase the employment of labor in menial service only, their profusion, or the expenditure of their annual income, is more promotive of the general interests of the nation than their savings from it would be ; for in the former case, the expenditure, by the distribution it makes of wealth, causes a portion of it to find its way into the hands of those engaged in productive industry, and there to be employed as capital to the increase of production ; whereas in the latter case, the savings would be retained for unproductive purposes, and the means would be less for the employment of productive labor. Further, it is an error to suppose, that whatever is expended is so much consumed. The rich man, in expending his annual income, neither consumes more food, nor wears more clothing, than he would, were his expenditure less. In expending his income for labor, or for the products of labor, as he does, money merely passes from hands, in which it was unproductive, to concentrate itself in hands, in which it becomes productive.

THE END.